TOOLS FOR ORGANIC FARMING

TOOLS FOR ORGANIC FARMING

A manual of appropriate equipment and treatments

Edited and introduced by George McRobie

Intermediate Technology Publications 1990

Acknowledgements

Intermediate Technology Development Group is indebted to Harold Pearson and Sir Julian Rose for their work in selecting and checking the technical content of this manual and to Simon Croxton for help with the Introduction. We are especially grateful to the Sainsbury Charitable Fund for a generous financial grant towards the research and publication costs of this manual.

Published by Intermediate Technology Publications,
103-105 Southampton Row, London WC1B 4HH, UK.

Published in North America by
The Bootstrap Press, an imprint of
the Intermediate Technology Development Group
of North America,
777 United Nations Plaza,
New York, NY 10017

ISBN 1 85339 009 7 (UK) ⁄
ISBN 1 942850 19 X (US)

Printed by the Russell Press Ltd., Bertrand Russell House, Gamble Street, Nottingham NG7 4ET, UK.

Contents

Introduction

This Manual's antecedents go back to the first days of the Intermediate Technology Development Group. Very soon after a few of us had helped E.F. Schumacher to form the Group, we produced *Tools for Progress*, a guide to relatively inexpensive equipment for small-scale and rural development. It included equipment for farming, manufacturing and processing. It was, of course, far from exhaustive, and some of the equipment may not have been exactly right for the rural poor. But it was of crucial importance because it served to focus attention on the fact, then far from widely understood, that the large-scale and expensive technology of the rich was no good for poor people in poor communities. To meet their needs a different technology had to be discovered or devised: small, simple, capital- and energy-saving, non-violent toward people and their environment. The enthusiasm with which *Tools for Progress* was received around the world left the Group in no doubt that it was on the right track.

A few years later, arising out of field programmes in Zambia and Nigeria, one section of the original guide was expanded into *Tools for Agriculture*, and, for people who could not afford to buy such tools but could get them made locally, details were provided of hand- and animal-drawn equipment that could be fabricated by local blacksmiths (and we included tools for blacksmiths, too).

Today, nearly twenty years on, IT Publication's list of titles on agriculture is as many as 24. But it is the content and not the number that matters. Virtually all the books relate to a style of farming very different from that of the rich industrial countries.

As far as aid and development policies are concerned, the shift in focus from large-scale farming on the industrialized-country model towards the small, mixed farm of the poor countries — and their only hope, indeed, of achieving food security and self-reliance — is not yet complete but is well under way. There is still, however, a very real danger that many developing countries are adopting many of the worst aspects of rich-country agriculture. It can hardly be over-emphasized that conventional agriculture in the North is essentially non-sustainable and it is very important for our survival that we get rid of its most violent aspects within the next generation. It is tragic that, just as a growing body of opinion in the rich North is starting to demand that agriculture takes a different route towards sustainable, ecologically based farming systems, and uncontaminated food and water, the poor countries of the world are increasingly being sold on the idea that the prevailing style of unsustainable, chemical-based farming is the answer to their food problems.

The two contrasting approaches to agriculture and food production, the chemical and the biological, essentially exemplify what is meant by inappropriate and appropriate technology.

There is in fact a parallel between the way that scientists and technologists first resorted to violent methods to try to ensure future supplies of two of the basic needs for mankind, energy and food. The reaction to a growing awareness of the finite nature of fossil fuels was to rush towards nuclear power. In the case of agriculture, the reaction to becoming more dependent on imports, or in some cases the lure of exporting more, led the rich countries of the North into a heedless rush towards chemical-based agriculture. The dramatic rise in the use of chemicals in agriculture started in the 1940s. Until about the late '60s the growth in world fertilizer use was concentrated in the rich countries, where it rose from 14 to 63 million tonnes between 1950 and 1970. Over the same period, energy use in agriculture (again concentrated in the rich countries) quadrupled. The rise in the use of nitrogen fertilizer, along with the growing trend towards cereal monocropping, are dominant trends of the past 40 years. Nitrogen fertilizer use in the UK rose from about 50,000 tonnes in 1940 to more than 1.2 million tonnes in 1980. Increased use of fertilizer is accompanied by increased use of pesticides and herbicides: the fertilizer encourages weeds, and also increases the plant's uptake of water, weakening its ability to resist disease and encouraging aphids and other pests: so herbicides and pesticides are brought in. As the soil becomes impoverished and some pests become resistant to current pesticides, more chemicals are employed.

Energy dependence on fossil fuels

Thus the agriculture that has developed in the North since the 1950s is one that has increasingly poured fossil fuel, mostly oil, onto the land, and has mined food energy from the land. The upshot is an unsustainable system of agriculture in energy terms. On both sides of the Atlantic, about three calories of energy are used for every one calorie of food obtained. If we add in the costs of processing, distribution and food preparation, the balance becomes much more unfavourable, more like 5:1 in Britain and nearer 10:1 in the USA.

Soil loss

This system is unsustainable environmentally; there is growing evidence of the degradation of soil and of soil erosion. In Britain the removal of hedges and the compaction of soil by heavy machinery contribute to soil degradation[1] and in the USA recent studies suggest that soil loss per acre is 25 to 50 per cent greater than it was in the 1930s when the Soil Conservation Service was set up.

Nitrates in water

There is growing concern about the effect of nitrates on human health. Between 40 and 50 per cent of the nitrate is leached from the soil each year,

2

and, because it takes many years for the nitrate to reach the water table, its concentration in water supplies is bound to get higher in the years ahead. The WHO limit for nitrate in water is 11.3mg per litre, above which there may be health problems. This limit is already often exceeded in water supplies from East Anglia in the UK, and in the same region concentrations well above 22mg per litre have been widely encountered under arable fields.[2]

But most of our nitrate intake is likely to come from the vegetables we eat. A recent study shows that some 70 per cent of average daily nitrate intake per person was from vegetables, compared with 21 per cent from water.[3] There is evidence that compost-grown plants have concentrates of nitrate only half that of plants grown with chemical fertilizers and incidentally, that the dry matter in a compost-grown plant is more than 20 per cent higher than in a chemically fertilized one — the consumer is getting better value. There is also evidence that organically grown food keeps better, and is more nutritious than chemically grown.[4]

Medical evidence of the precise dangers of nitrates is not conclusive, but it would be as well to keep our intake as low as possible, not least because of the many other industrial chemicals in food.

Pesticide pollution

In the mid-1980s about 30 million tonnes of pesticides were used in Britain: herbicides accounted for 65 per cent, fungicides for 21 per cent and insecticides for 6 per cent. There is growing public concern about both the health and environmental hazards of pesticide use. In a recent study the widely respected London Food Commission notes:

> In a survey of 1,649 fruit and vegetable samples analysed for residues between 1981 and 1984, 43 per cent contained detectable residues even though the tests used could not have identified all the residues which could have been present. Particularly worrying were the 29 samples which contained residues at levels which indicated misuse . . . high DDT levels found on vegetables indicated that its use continued after it had been totally banned in Britain . . . even suppliers who, as signatories to the voluntary approval scheme, might be expected to observe it, have sold pesticides for which approval has been withdrawn . . .[5]

Studies have implicated at least 49 pesticides as possibly causing cancer, at least 31 as possibly causing birth defects, and at least 61 as possibly causing genetic defects. Many under each heading — some 40 are named by the Commission — are still widely used in Britain. The Commission strongly criticizes the statutory control planned under the Food and Environment Protection Act 1985, because, for instance, of a very small increase (7.5 per cent) in the inspectorate, and because 'analysis by either government or local authorities would identify and measure only a minimal proportion of the 426 active ingredients currently cleared for use'.[6]

There is growing doubt about whether the pesticides are really effective. It has been estimated that while insecticide use rose ten-fold in the USA in the 30 years up to 1974, pre-harvest insect losses actually rose, from about 7 per cent

3

to 13 per cent. Of the 25 most serious pests in California, 24 have been reported to be either insecticide aggravated or actually insecticide induced — these pests whose harmful effects have either been exacerbated or have only been noted after natural predators have been eliminated by pesticide use.[7] The growing resistance of many pests to pesticides is another problem — the number of pesticide-resistant species world-wide rose from 25 in 1974 to 432 in 1980.[8]

Pesticides in the Third World

Similar problems are beginning to emerge in developing countries. Although they did not start using fertilizers and pesticides on any scale until around 1970, in the next decade their use of fertilizers grew twice as fast as in the North; the FAO forecast future growth to the year 2000 at about 8 per cent a year. As to pesticides, by the mid-1980s USA and western Europe accounted for about half the world market, and the developing countries for between 25 and 30 per cent. Already, then, the developing countries are exposed to the hazards of agro-chemicals. *The Report to the World Commission on Environment and Development* states: '. . . because of the larger populations exposed, the greater institutional and educational barriers to safe use and the higher rates of inter-farm spill-overs stemming from the smaller-farm pattern prevalent in developing countries, the problems of pollution and contamination could reach or exceed those of developed countries'.[9]

Although data are unreliable, it is estimated that some 10,000 people die each year in developing countries and about 400,000 suffer acutely from pesticide poisoning. Many pesticides are concentrated as they move up the food chain. PCNBs (pentachloronitrobenzenes) are found in many people in the North; and in countries such as China and India, where persistent organo-chlorine compounds are in use, medium concentrations in the fat of mothers' milk indicate that the milk exceeds the danger limits set by the World Health Organization.[10]

Problems of over-production

In the rich industrialized countries, particularly Europe and North America, during the past 30 years the rapid development of oil-based, industrialized agriculture along with vast farm subsidies, has produced a truly formidable array of problems:

○ Resources are wasted producing surplus food, and disposing of it. In 1987 the EEC spent £16 billion — two-thirds of its budget — on the Common Agricultural Policy, most of it to buy surpluses which are then exported at subsidized prices, or destroyed. In 1984, for instance, Michael Montague, Chairman of the National Consumer Council, stated (according to the London Food Commission) that 5,000 unsold oranges, 5,000 lemons and 40 cauliflowers were destroyed *every minute*.

○ Big farms have benefited more than small; rising land prices, along with the cost of modern equipment, have inhibited new entrants into farming; and the rural population has steadily declined.

○ Farming is no longer in harmony with other rural life because of its side-effects on the wild-life and the beauty and amenity of the countryside.

○ Agricultural policies of the rich countries are·damaging to the developing countries, both by the export of subsidized farm produce and by promoting an oil-based, unsustainable agriculture in poor countries.

○ There is growing concern about food quality within the rich countries, especially its contamination by pesticides, herbicides and nitrates, and concern about the contamination of water supplies.

○ There is also concern about soil erosion and soil quality; dependence on fossil fuels; and about animal welfare, and the loss of genetic variety in agriculture.

The reversal of these trends would, in fact, constitute the basis of a rational agricultural policy, and while organic farming would not overcome all of the problems set out above, it would unquestionably solve many of them — notably those related to the devastating costs of huge subsidies and huge surpluses; soil preservation and quality; food quality and safety; and unsustainability on energy and environmental grounds. Organic farming, that is, can be the basis of a sane, sustainable and publicly acceptable agricultural policy. There would be other spin-offs, such as more employment. A German study concluded a few years ago that if West German farmers all converted to organic methods they would produce some 25 per cent less, increase their net proceeds, benefit people and the environment — and also create more than 1.5 million new jobs.[11]

Organic farming — the sustainable production system

The present crisis of over-production in the North offers a unique opportunity for building organic farming into agricultural policy.

In agriculture the appropriate technology is biological (generally referred to as organic) husbandry, an agricultural system based on ecological principles, in which external inputs are minimized and chemicals such as fertilizers, pesticides and herbicides are not used, and which treat the soil as a living organism to be nurtured and kept healthy.[12]

In Europe the discussion about how to cut surpluses and subsidies centres on how to compensate farmers for growing less. One way is to grow less per hectare; another is to plant fewer hectares. The conventional objection to either course of action is that they would raise farmers' costs: and so they would, other things remaining the same. But a policy of encouraging farmers to convert to organic (and existing organic farmers to use more land for green manures) could both reduce production by some 20 per cent, and (given a few years for the conversion) leave farmers with a higher gross margin than before. This is because their costs will be cut by eliminating chemicals, and because there is a premium paid for organic produce: so a cut of 20 per cent in their output will be more than matched by the reduction in their costs and the rise in their revenue. (Experience shows that, a few years after converting to organic methods a farmer will produce about 20 per cent less than he did when using chemicals.)[13]

Today the organic movement in Britain is growing in strength and influence. Several of the biggest food stores, notably Sainsbury, Safeways and Waitrose, are already stocking organic produce to Soil Association Standards, and other major retailers are likely to express their preference for the Soil Association symbol quality products.

The Soil Association, the leading advocate of the organic movement, is extending the use of its symbol to processors, wholesalers and retailers as well as growers, and has recently launched 'The Living Earth' movement to involve consumers in the drive towards uncontaminated food and a healthy environment. There are now 400 symbol holders and it is internationally recognized as the guarantee of a rigorous standard of organic quality. Several other complementary organizations promoting the organic approach and comprising practitioners and supporters include the Henry Doubleday Research Association, primarily for gardeners and horticulturalists, the British Organic Farmers, the Organic Growers' Association, and the Organic Farmers' and Growers' Co-operative. There are vigorous organic movements elsewhere in Europe and the United States, and everywhere the demand for organic foods is outstripping supply.

Many farmers and growers now make a good living from organic food production, but it remains true that there is no easily available body of economic and scientific information about organic farming. Much of the work that has been done has come from Switzerland and West Germany, and a lot of it is either inaccessible or not very useful to the average British farmer. Notable work, especially for gardeners and smallholders, is done by Henry Doubleday; and the Elm Farm Research Institute, also privately funded, is producing valuable material from its scientific research on organic farming and methods of conversion from chemical to organic farming. In 1980 they studied the research needs of organic farmers in the UK, and found that research was most urgent in the areas of crop rotations; methods of nitrogen supply through legumes; manure management; weed control; and appropriate cultivation methods. What is now badly needed is what Dr Hardy Vogtmann, professor of alternative agriculture at the University of Kassel, W. Germany, has called research 'directed towards a better understanding of agro-ecosystems and how to maintain them, rather than towards the destruction or replacement of biological systems with more energy-consuming industrial methods'. This is essentially multidisciplinary research with a farming-systems perspective.[14]

In its Organic Manifesto presented to Parliament in June 1987, the Soil Association called for action on the part of Government to:

○ subsidize the conversion period needed to develop organic farming;

○ back the organic standards agreed on and administered by the Soil

Association;
○ extend the environmentally sensitive areas management scheme to include organic farms;
○ increase the facilities for teaching organic farming;
○ set up an experimental programme for scientific and economic research into organic farming;
○ assess the role of organic methods in aid projects.

At the time of writing, it seems that the Ministry of Agriculture and the Agricultural and Food Research Council are by no means unsympathetic to these objectives. (A similar change in the climate of official opinion appears to be taking place in the USA, for example with the federally funded programme for Appropriate Technology Transfer to Rural Areas.) Governments are recognizing that organic farming could make a major positive contribution to the problems of agricultural surpluses, food quality, and environmental protection.

In developing countries, too, the spread of chemicals — although unquestionably increasing yields — is giving rise to serious reservations. Thus Dr M.S. Swaminathan, then Director-General of the International Rice Research Institute and President of the International Union for the Conservation of Nature and Natural Resources, in the course of an outstanding address to the Royal Society of Arts on global agriculture, makes frequent reference to the need to preserve biological systems and the dangers of going for short-term gains at the expense of sustainability. He concludes '... The global food scenario is one of hope on the production front. However, it is one of despair both in the field of equitable distribution and sustainability of the production pathways adopted. The very success on the production front provides us with an opportunity to correct the deficiencies in the other areas'. He called for an international organization '... to help monitor avoidable damage to life-support systems due to either political or commercial greed or careless technology'.[15]

In 1976, in an address to the Soil Association, E.F. Schumacher asked what should be expected of agriculture during the next 30 years. He argued for food self-sufficiency, for healthy food based on organic methods, for a major expansion in agro-forestry; and he emphasized that there are other tasks for agriculture no less important: maintenance of soil quality and an agreeable and healthy landscape; the maintenance of genetic variety, of pure water supplies, and of rural communities. Twelve years on, there are heartening signs of a wider public and political recognition of this role for agriculture: that its importance goes far beyond providing cheap food for cities.

A wise old market gardener once told me that in his youth, when French market gardeners had to move for any reason, they loaded their topsoil into carts and took it with them. If so, they knew what they were about: the living earth they had spent years building up was just as valuable an asset as the skill in their own minds and hands. What I have tried to show in this brief introduction is that there are now some solid reasons for believing that we are

7

in the midst of a major shift in opinion about agriculture on the part of farmers and the public, both professionals and politicians. It is a shift towards the understanding that the soil-plant-animal-man relationship can be broken only at our peril; that if we treat the living earth properly, we can move towards an economically sustainable agriculture, healthy food, and a healthy environment.

This change is only just beginning — just as the deficiencies of the trickle-down theory of economic development were only just beginning to be revealed when the Intermediate Technology Development Group was formed. In the case of agriculture, too, the need for and the possibilities of changing from chemical to biological methods did not come about by itself: it is the result of many years of effort on the part of practical farmers and others who formed bodies such as the Soil Association and its counterparts around the world, more recently joined by environmentalists and concerned health workers.

Again, on a parallel with the IT Group in the 1960s, there is today a pressing need for a new kind of research and development effort. Before organic farming can become widespread, the norm rather than the exception, much new work is needed on agro-ecology and biological systems. A groundwork of knowledge has been put in place by the efforts of individual farmers and exceptional scientists, and through research done in privately funded centres such as Elm Farm and Emerson College in Britain, universities in Germany, Netherlands and Switzerland, and at several places in the USA, including the Rodale Research Institute, the Land Institute, and the universities of Santa Barbara and especially Michigan State. But whereas most of the research into chemicals, and a lot of work on chemical farming, has been financed by a handful of agro-industries in support of a billion-pound market, the research and extension work needed to upgrade and widen the practice of organic farming does not result in patentable products that appeal to big business: it provides information and knowledge. And while the free market has many virtues, to leave this kind of research to the market would qualify for Galbraith's description of running the economy without the intervention of human intelligence. Only a government-funded programme of research and development and extension can bring about the transformation of British agriculture that is needed during the next decade.

The starting point of a thorough-going programme of research and development designed to promote organic farming would be close consultation with organizations that represent the interests of organic farmers in different ways. The adoption of the Soil Association symbol — which has gained international respect for its rigorous standards of quality and practice, would be an immediate first step, because this clearly delineates what farmers are to be encouraged to convert to: and makes clear the quality standards which wholesalers, retailers and consumers can feel confident about.

An early phase of the programme would be a detailed study, both agro-ecological and economic, of existing organic farming systems in Britain. This would provide a data base for use both in teaching, and to identify areas for further investigation. It would also help to establish the duration of the conversion period during which, while the soil recovers its life and fertility, subsidy will be required. How do we express the values that must be attached to the sustainability of soil and food quality, the well-being of animals and men? This will call for some new thinking on the part of conventional economists. A study of this nature would be a precondition of the R. & D. phase of the programme, which will require the setting up of a research farm, and also on-farm research involving commercial farms, universities and existing research organizations such as Elm Farm, Henry Doubleday, and Emerson College.

Particular areas of activity about which much more must be learnt and data disseminated include the design of rotations and the effect on soil fertility and weed control of different rotations and different soils. Effective methods of weed control by cultivation must be explored, and also improved methods of fertilizer and manure application. The least-cost access by farmers to all available forms of organic plant nutrients will have to be made available. In the interests of local rural communities and of farm incomes, local processing of farm outputs will have to be explored. Processing, and the supply of farm inputs, should increasingly come under the control of farmers and local communities. Work done with small farmers in the USA has demonstrated that farmers can also reduce their energy costs by up to 30 per cent without adopting any kind of complex technology.

Particular attention will have to be given to the availability of technological choice. As a general rule, and left, so to speak, to the free play of market forces, R. & D. programmes tend to favour the big against the small, the rich against the poor, the centralized against the decentralized. It is one of the experiences of Intermediate Technology that a special kind of effort is needed to ensure that not only the big and medium, but also and especially the small farmer has access to technology appropriate to his needs and resources, using the term technology to embrace everything from the quality of seeds and other inputs, knowledge of the best practice, or the hardware associated with the processes of ground preparation, planting, cultivation, harvesting, processing and marketing. We also share the knowledge with dozens of other appropriate technology groups around the world that it is perfectly feasible to discover or devise technologies to meet most peoples' needs. If engineers are asked to devise tools and equipment that are small-scale, efficient, skill- rather than capital-intensive, they will generally rise to the challenge.

This manual is offered as a small contribution towards part of the research that is needed into a technology for organic farming. Like its forebear, *Tools for Progress*, it does not pretend to be exhaustive. It is intended to serve the needs of the small- to medium-scale organic farmer in Britain, Europe and the USA. The items in it have the merit of having been selected by practical farmers. Its very gaps in coverage may well indicate where more practical research and development is needed. I hope that it will be the start of a series that will increasingly augment the technology of organic agriculture both in the North and the South; and that we shall shortly see manuals for other countries, different crops or perhaps climatic regions. But wherever it may lead, *Tools for Organic Farming* is a good beginning.

George McRobie
London

References

1. C. Arden-Clarke and R.D. Hodges, 'Soil Erosion in Britain', *Biological Agriculture and Horticulture*, Vol.4, No.4, 1987.
2. Some nitrate leaking would also occur with organic farming, but good husbandry would keep it well within acceptable levels.
3. D. Hodges, 'Agriculture, Nitrates and Health', *Soil Association Review*, September 1985.
4. See D. Lairon *et al*, 'Analysis of Vegetables Produced by Orthodox and Biological Methods: Some preliminary results', in B. Stonehouse *Biological Husbandry*, Butterworths, 1981.
5. Pete Snell, *Pesticide Residues and Food: The Case for Real Control*, The London Food Commission, 1986. See also Nigel Dudley, *This Poisoned Earth*, Piatkus, London, 1987.
6. Pete Snell, *op.cit.*
7. Pete Snell, *op.cit.*
8. *Food 2000, Report to the World Commission on Environment and Development*, Zed Books, London 1987, p.40.
9. *Food 2000, op.cit.*, pp.39, 40.
10. *Food 2000, op.cit.*
11. W. Wiesers, reported in *Frankfurter Rundshau*, 15 May 1984.
12. 'A low external-input system', as defined by the International Federation of Organic Agriculture Movements, includes the following objectives:
    ○ Organization of the production of crops and livestock and management of farm resources so that they harmonize rather than conflict with natural systems.
    ○ Development and use of appropriate technologies based on the understanding of biological systems.
    ○ Achievement and maintenance of soil fertility for optimum production by relying primarily on renewable resources.
    ○ Diversification for optimum production.
    ○ Pursuit of optimum nutritional value of staple foods.
    ○ Decentralization of structures for processing, distributing and marketing produce.
    ○ Maintenance of equitable relationships between those who work and live on the land.
    ○ Creation of a system that is aesthetically pleasing for those working in the system and those viewing it from outside.
    ○ Maintenance and preservation of wildlife and their habitats.
    Cited by Dr Hardy Vogtmann in *Sustainable Agriculture and Integrated Farming Systems*, Michigan State University Press, 1985.
13. *Options for Encouraging the Expansion of Organic Agriculture through the Extensification Scheme*, Elm Farm Research Centre, 1988.
14. Simon Croxton, 'The Costs and Benefits of Converting to Organic Systems: and Assessment of Research Requirements', MSc thesis paper, Silsoe, 1987.
15. Dr M.S. Swathinathan, 'The Emerging Global Agricultural Scenario', *Royal Society of Arts Journal*, London, November 1987.

1. Crop protection

The protection of crops against pests and diseases in an organic farming system requires a very different approach to that found in conventional agriculture. In the latter, the farmers have at their disposal a wide range of chemical pesticides which are used to combat the organisms — bacteria, fungi, insects — which may be attacking the crops. However, as has been mentioned in the introduction to this manual, forty years of increasingly sophisticated chemical crop-protection strategies have not necessarily resulted in more effective pest and disease control, nor in significant reductions in crop losses caused by these agents. Problems such as pesticide resistance, the development of secondary pests, the pollution of food and water by residues, and damage to a wide range of non-pest organisms are now widely accepted as arising directly as a result of pesticide use.

The organic farmers' approach to crop protection is essentially a biological rather than a chemical one. They attempt to control pests and diseases by developing and enhancing some of a whole range of natural, biological processes and cycles that occur in and around the farm ecosystem and by combining these with a variety of cultural controls and the use of biodegradable pesticides, most of which are of natural origin.

Although it has not yet been clearly demonstrated scientifically, a recurring experience of organic farmers in the field is that their crops do not suffer pests and diseases to the same extent as would be found in an equivalent conventionally produced crop. This can be explained largely on the basis of the differences between the ways in which crop nutrients are supplied in the two systems. One of the main principles of organic husbandry is that plant nutrients are not fed direct to the plant roots in an easily soluble form, as happens with chemical fertilizers in conventional farming. Instead the technique is to 'feed the soil' either with manures, composts or other organic materials, or with relatively insoluble sources of nutrients such as rock dusts (e.g. rock phosphate), so that plant nutrients have to be cycled through the active microbial biomass within the soil before they become available to the crop roots. In this way, the crops' needs are made available to them in a balanced form, with adequate supplies of major, minor and trace elements, but with none in excess.

On the other hand, conventional agriculture normally only applies fertilizers containing the major nutrients, nitrogen, phosphorus and potash, leaving other nutrients to be supplied from soil reserves. Application of the large amounts of N, P and K required to produce maximum productivity may imbalance other nutrients within the soil or within the crop, particularly because of the very soluble, and thus highly available, form in which the fertilizers are applied. These imbalances can make the plants more susceptible to pests and diseases leading them to require regular applications of pesticides to prevent significant losses.

This generally lower incidence of pest and disease attacks in organically produced crops means that crop protection in an organic system does not have to be so specific as that in a conventional system. The holistic approach being followed on an organic farm should result in an ecological balance within the system which, combined with a balanced nutrition for the crops, will prevent serious pest outbreaks much of the time. Such an approach will result in many pest and disease organisms being present in individual crops without them necessarily rising to levels where they cause economic damage. Thus, provided that quality requirements do not insist that the produce should be totally free of damage, organic crop-protection methods are frequently only a relatively minor part of the overall system, rather than a regular series of sprays throughout the life of a crop, as is found in conventional farming. Having said this, it must be recognized that from time to time, for a variety of reasons, organic crops will suffer significant attacks from pests or diseases which will need to be controlled, and for which acceptable methods must be available.

Protection techniques

Organic farming is a systems approach, not a piecemeal approach, to food production. Thus many of the techniques of crop protection will consist of integrated aspects of a holistic system rather than particular responses to specific problems in individual crops. For example, whilst the conventional farmer will spray fungicide on a growing wheat crop in response to the development of a fungus disease, the organic farmer seeks to ensure that the ecological and nutritional balance within the farm and the soil will enable the crop to resist the disease so that significant yield loss does not occur. Major aspects of the system which are directly correlated with crop protection are described in the paragraphs which follow.

The soil

The development and maintenance of a biologically active and fertile soil, mainly by increasing organic matter levels through the recycling of manures, organic wastes, etc., preferably via the process of composting, will have the following direct or indirect impacts upon the levels of pests and diseases:
○ The improved soil structure, and the soil drainage, aeration, and water-holding capacity resulting from increased levels of organic matter, will result in well-developed rooting systems and healthier and more disease-resistant crops.
○ The balanced nutrition supplied by a biologically fertile soil produces crops which are normally more resistant to pests and diseases than when

fertilizers are used to provide nutrients. The availability to crops of high levels of fertilizer nitrogen will tend to produce more lush growth, increased amounts of certain non-protein nitrogen compounds in the plant sap, and a reduction in the levels of protective secondary metabolites, such as phenols, and this will leave the plants more susceptible to pests and diseases.

○ There is specific evidence that a whole range of organic amendments can help to control soil-borne crop diseases. Amendments such as manures stimulate increased populations of soil micro-organisms, and these interact to limit the development or activity of pathogenic bacteria or fungi.

The environment

One of the priorities when starting an organic farm should be the development and maintenance, to the greatest degree possible, of an ecological balance within the environment in and around the farm. In general terms, human agricultural activities tend to simplify the natural ecosystems upon which they are imposed, and in the most intensive modern farming systems this may result in the environment becoming grossly simplified in both time and space — as in the widespread continuous monocropping of arable crops such as wheat. Natural, climax ecosystems are highly complex, balanced systems with considerable inherent stability. Simplification, as a result of human interference, results in increasing instability in these ecosystems. In conventional farming this tendency towards simplification in pursuit of 'efficiency', plus the nutritional imbalances resulting from fertilizer use, has given rise to an increased susceptibility to pests and diseases plus a reduced potential for natural pest control. The result has been more crop problems and the greater need for pesticides.

The organic alternative to this is to attempt to develop as wide a natural diversity across the farm as possible, so that significant populations of predators and pest- and disease-antagonistic organisms are maintained, either in focal areas from which they can spread out or as general, low-level populations, available to respond to the development of any outbreak on the farm. Thus, the organic farmer will seek to maintain as high a level of ecological complexity as possible and not to simplify the farm ecosystem more than is absolutely necessary. The following practices are of value in this:

○ Organic farms are preferably mixed farms, with several crop and animal systems in operation in any season and a complex rotational system operating over a cycle of several years. This complexity approximates as closely as possible, in the relatively artificial conditions of agriculture, to the highly intricate organization of a natural ecosystem, and in this way it develops a stability and structure whereby pest and disease populations are unable to build up to excessive levels and where moderate numbers of control organisms are maintained in readiness for pest outbreaks.

○ Small areas of natural woodland scattered over the farm and hedges surrounding the fields will provide areas where predators can maintain focal populations in readiness to act against any developing pest outbreaks, and also to provide sites for the over wintering of these organisms. These woods and hedgerows should be as ecologically complex as possible in order to provide the necessary habitats for maintaining a range of predator species.

○ In areas where predator species need to be particularly concentrated, their presence can be enhanced by introducing plots of plants which are attractive to predators in various ways. For example, the planting of an understorey of umbelliferous plants in orchards will attract hover-flies and parasitic wasps.

This environmental approach to organic pest and disease control means that the farmer is best served by having, if possible, a detailed understanding of the natural history of the area in which the farm is sited and, in particular, a knowledge of the main pest and disease organisms and their antagonists. Such knowledge will enable these natural checks and balances to be integrated into the structure of the farm and its rotational system.

Cropping systems

Diversity is probably the most important factor when considering crop protection in organic cropping systems. Extensive mono-cropping is not acceptable since it increases the likelihood of pest and disease outbreaks. Small to moderate areas of individual crops integrated into a rotation where similar crops are not grown in the same field for more than one or two seasons consecutively, will help prevent pest build-up. Other approaches which can help to enhance crop protection are:

○ Mixed planting of several strains of, for example, barley with different capabilities of disease-resistance provides better natural disease control within the crop. It frequently also results in increased yields when compared with the pure strains.

○ Companion planting of two different crop species in blocks or rows together can integrate the pests and disease-controlling properties of one to the advantage of the other.[1]

Organic pesticides and control agents

If the methods described above do not inhibit pest or disease outbreaks, then it is necessary to use one or more of a small range of organically acceptable control agents. Most synthetic chemical pesticides as used in conventional agriculture are unacceptable in organic systems, but there are a number of biological control agents, natural pesticides and other chemicals which, because of their biodegradability, low general toxicity, low environmental impact, or their specificity, are acceptable for use in organic farming.[2] The most commonly used and reliable of these materials are as follows (all these preparations are available from the Henry Doubleday Research Association[3]):

Derris dust A powdered, plant-based insecticide effective against aphids, caterpillars, weevils, and a range of other insects.

Derris-Pyrethrum spray A liquid insecticide for the control of aphids, caterpillars, thrips, and other insect pests. Harmful to bees and other beneficial insects, so it needs careful use.

Insecticidal soap Controls aphids, whitefly, spider mites, etc. Safe to wildlife, including bees and ladybirds.

Quassia chips An extract of this plant material can be used to control aphids, sawflies, caterpillars, etc. Harmless to bees and ladybirds.

Koppert's natural fungicide A sulphur spray for the control of black spot, powdery mildew, and scab diseases. Needs careful use as it can harm some natural biological control organisms.

Bordeaux mixture A traditional copper fungicide used as a preventative against potato blight and to control fungal diseases of fruit.

Bacillus thuringiensis (Bactospeine W.P.) A bacterial preparation which controls cabbage caterpillars and cabbage moth, as well as a number of other lepidopterous pests.

Encarsia formosa A parasitic wasp used to control whitefly in glasshouses.

Phytoseilus persimilis For the control of red spider mite in glasshouses.

Trappit Codling Moth trap A pheromone trap for helping to control codling moth in fruit.

Trichoderma viride (Binab T) This fungal agent is sold as a control for silver leaf disease of fruit trees (*Chondrostereum purpureum*), but has also been claimed to control Dutch elm disease (*Ceratocystis ulmi*), tree stem and root rot (*Heterobasidion annosum*) and honey fungus (*Armillaria mellea*).[4]

The position regarding microbiological control agents for pests and diseases is well-summarized by Lynch and Hobbie.[4]

Weed control

Although not, strictly speaking, an aspect of crop protection, weed control is a very important consideration in organic crop production and thus merits a mention here. In an organic system weeds are more than just things that have to be controlled in order to obtain a good crop; they also provide information to the farmer about the condition of the soil. According to the type and balance of weed species in a field, it is possible to determine whether the soil is fertile, too acid, compacted, and so on.[5]

The control of weeds is not just a simple activity, such as spraying a herbicide at certain times in the crop cycle; it is a complex operation which is at least partially integrated with other aspects of the whole farm operation. The following are the most important stages:[5]

○ The control of weed seeds. By good manure and compost management, and the control of weeds elsewhere, weed seeds should be prevented from coming on to the cropped fields.

○ Taking a weed-strike. The preparation of a seed bed about two weeks before the crop is due to be sown enables the farmer to kill any early germinating weeds by harrowing immediately prior to sowing the crop.

○ Mechanical and thermal weed control. At various stages in the crop's growth, weeds may be controlled by both thermal and mechanical methods. The latter is usually by tractor-mounted steerage hoes and spring-tine hoes.

○ Some hand hoeing may be necessary, particularly for in-row weeding of some crops.

Weed control is also an important point to be taken into account when considering the design of the overall farm rotation. Considerable control or suppression of weed populations can result from the correct juxtaposition of crops in a rotation. Conversely, weed population build-up can result from poorly designed rotations.

D. Hodges
Wye College, University of London

References

1. H. Philbrick and R.B. Gregg, *Companion Plants*, London, Watkins, 1979.
2. 'Standards for Organic Agriculture', The Soil Association, 86 Colston Street, Bristol BS1 5BB.
3. The Henry Doubleday Research Association, National Centre for Organic Gardening, Ryton Gardens, Ryton-on-Dunsmore, Coventry CV8 3LG.
4. J.M. Lynch and J.E. Hobbie, *Micro-organisms in Action: Concepts and Applications in Microbial Ecology*, Oxford, Blackwell, 1988, pp.261-87.
5. F. Blake, *The Handbook of Organic Husbandry*, Marlborough, The Crowood Press, 1987.

2. Seed-bed preparation and intercultivation

Soil is cultivated in order to provide good conditions in which seeds will germinate and plants will grow to achieve maximum yields. These are effected by:

○ Opening the soil structure for easy root development and the infiltration of water.

○ Cutting weed roots and burying green material to reduce crop losses from weed competition.

○ Incorporating manure.

Of all the agricultural tasks, cultivation can be the most demanding of time and energy; therefore it should not exceed the level necessary for the crop to thrive in a given soil, climate or farming system. For annual rain-fed crops the prime consideration is usually to establish plants as early as possible to achieve the longest possible growing season.

The time available for cultivation and planting depends upon the soil type, climate and cropping schedules.

In areas where, early in the season, water is not a limiting factor, the control

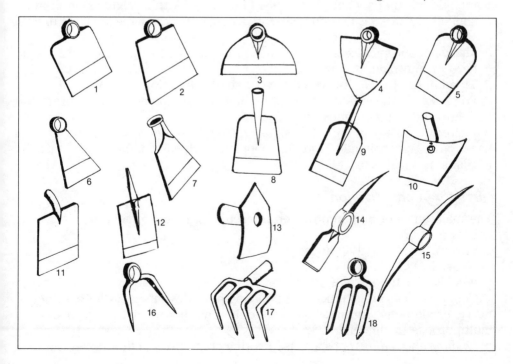

of weed growth is the principal problem. Poor weed control resulting from inadequate tillage can later force farmers to abandon their crops if the weeding techniques are unable to cope with the growth rate over the total area.

Hoes for primary tillage

Hoes are probably the most widely used tillage implement in the world. The range of forms that have been evolved in different regions (of which a limited sample is illustrated on p.17), reflects both varying local conditions such as soil and climate, and the specific needs of a people engaged in the cultivation of a certain crop or crops.

The hoes shown on p.17 are essentially primary tillage implements and are designed mainly for soil digging work. However, hoes are used for many other purposes, particularly weeding, ridging, bund forming and so on. They are the essential primary tool of hoe-farming cultures in which they are used for most farming operations. Initially they may be used to clear land of large weeds, in a scything action; to turn the soil over to bury the smaller weeds; to knock down the clods of earth to form a seed-bed; or to mound up the soil into planting hills; to open the soil to plant (particularly) large vegetative material; to weed; to mound up or ridge; to make irrigation bunds and channels and to divert irrigation water on to plots. The hoes in the illustration can be divided into three main categories:

○ Digging hoes which are used with a double-handed chopping action. These include the ring socket blade hoes (1-6), hoes with straight open or solid sockets (7, 8, 10, 11, 13) and hoes with a tang onto which the shaft is fitted (9, 12).
○ Mattocks and pickaxes (14, 15) which are useful for heavy duty work on hard or unbroken ground.
○ Tined hoes (16, 17, 18) which have a similar function to forks.

The boxes at the end of the chapter show a selection of manufacturers and indicates the range of hoes available.

There are so many varied designs of hoe that the classification used is necessarily approximate. Hoes appropriate to local conditions are usually available in local markets.

Hoes for intercultivation

The main types of human-powered intercultivating equipment are:
○ chopping hoes;
○ pushing and/or pulling hoes;
○ rotary hoes;
○ wheeled push hoes and cultivators.

Chopping hoes are similar to the digging hoes described earlier and indeed many smallholder farmers possess only one hoe which they use as a multipurpose implement.

Pushing and pulling hoes are used with a continuous action rather than the tiring intermittent strokes of a chopping hoe but are less suitable for hard soils, which they cannot easily penetrate. The blade is set at a sharper angle to the handle (about 55° to 65°, rather than 75° or so for a chopping hoe) so that the hoe blade is nearly horizontal.

Rotary hand weeders are used for crops grown on friable soils. In such cases the wheels are usually of peg or star-wheel form.

Wheeled push hoes and cultivators are available with a wide range of attachments — hoes, tines and mouldboards. They are particularly useful in friable loam or sandy soils for crops such as vegetables grown in narrow rows.

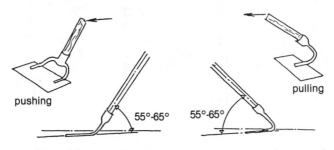

Pushing and pulling hoes, showing working angles.

Spades, forks and rakes

Spades are tools which are used for digging and turning soil. Unlike shovels, which are essentially materials-handling implements, spades will be subjected to considerable strain when being used for land-preparation work such as digging. This is reflected in their structure. The head of a spade will be made of a thicker and more tensile metal than would be found in a shovel head, and will have a slightly dished cross-section. The socket, where the head joins the shaft, will reflect a need to resist the high bending forces generated during soil turning and digging.

Forks used for seed-bed preparation may be divided into two groups according to prong shape and cross-section. A spade-fork (also called digging fork) is a heavy-duty implement with spatulated prongs used in a similar way and for similar functions as a spade. Ordinary digging or garden forks are distinguished by slender prongs which can be circular, triangular or square in section, although they are no less robust than the spade-fork. Their functions may include both primary (soil turning) or secondary (clod breaking) tillage operations.

Rakes are the hand-tool equivalent of the harrow and are used for secondary tillage of the seed-bed once it has been prepared with spades, hoes or forks. They are more lightly made than spades and forks, and are most often equipped with either an open socket (a split cylindrical collar into which the shaft is fitted secured by one or more screws) or tang-and-ferrule attachment (in which the shaft is placed on to the pointed tang and secured by the ferrule)

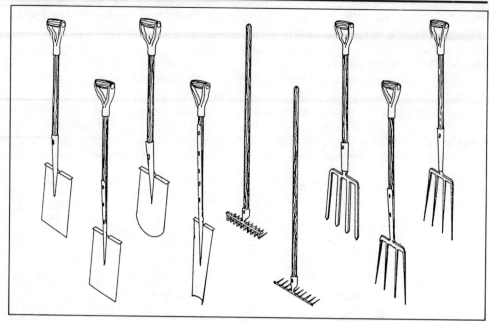

From left: solid socket treaded spade; strapped treaded spade; open socket treaded round nose spade; strapped treaded drainage spade; shaped-tine rake; garden rake; tang and ferrule broad-tine digging fork; strapped fork; solid socket digging fork.

Manufacturer	*Item*	*Other features*	*No. of models*
Bulldog Tools	Digging spade	Tread	13
UK	All metal spade	Tread	13
	Digging fork		6
	Turning fork		6
	Tang and ferrule rake	11 tine	3
Burgon and Ball			6
UK			6
			6
			6
			3
Caldwells	Treaded spade	3 rivet	11
UK	Export spade	3 rivet	11
	Digging fork	3 rivet	5
	Trenching fork	5 rivet	5
	Garden rake	12 tine	2
Neill Tools Ltd	Digging fork		4
Spear and Jackson division	Medium form		2
Tools — UK	Digging spade	Tread	12
	Irish spade	Tread	12
	Garden rake	12 tine	5

to the shaft. Rakes may be used for a variety of tasks including clod breaking, bed levelling and stone removal.

The table opposite lists a selection of spade, fork and rake manufacturers.

Animal-powered cultivation

Primary tillage This is carried out on open compacted soil after a fallow or seasonal cropping, thus allowing soil aeration to assist root development and the release of nutrients, and easing the passage of water into the soil, preventing wasteful run-off. Animal-powered equipment available for this operation includes traditional ploughs, as well as steel ploughs and associated implements.

Secondary tillage This is the formation of tilth in preparation for planting and inter-row weed control. It is necessary to place seeds at a specified depth in contact with a fine tilth and to cover them. A cloddy soil will lead to poor germination, but too fine a surface could allow soil capping between infrequent showers, leading to poor emergence.

Small seeds need a finer seed-bed and are often broadcast which does not allow subsequent mechanized weed control. Larger seeds are more easily planted in rows and the labour for weed control during the season is minimized.

Secondary tillage can be carried out with drag harrows, tines, or disc harrows. The drag harrows have a steel or wooden frame fitted with steel pegs, and weight can be added to the frame to aid penetration. Disc harrows are often fitted with a seat for the operator, whose weight automatically assists penetration. However, discs are generally more expensive than other forms of secondary tillage equipment.

Rigid or spring tines can be used in threes or fives for secondary cultivation. Although the speed at which oxen can cultivate is too low for spring tines to achieve soil shatter, their use does provide protection when obstacles are struck: the whole draught capacity can be imposed on a single tine when an obstacle is struck, so the tine and its attachment to the frame have to be capable of withstanding it.

Land forming Control and efficient utilization of water are a basic requirement of both rain-fed and irrigated agriculture.

On land with a slope in excess of 5 per cent, heavy storms can cause soil erosion, and in severe cases fields can be totally degraded in three to four years. Conventional cultivation should be avoided on slopes over 12 per cent.

Below 12 per cent, ridgers can provide satisfactory water and soil conservation. The ridges should be aligned close to the contours, and an incline of 0.5 to 2 per cent provides adequate drainage. Where storms are heavy but infrequent the ridges can be tied, i.e. joined by a cross ridge at intervals of two to three metres, to hold back water in the furrow. The proper alignment of ridges is essential, because low points in a furrow can flood and break out from the side of the ridge, and this is then repeated down the slope.

The production of crops on ridges is also often recommended where soil erosion is not a problem. Their use can be justified in areas which become waterlogged, so that the plants are above the water inundation level and as such are suitable for flood irrigation; but where these conditions do not exist, cropping on the flat is normally preferable because weed control is easier.

The maintenance required for simple tillage implements is minimal. Bolts and nuts should be kept tight; oil applied to threads will ease the removal of nuts when replacing parts. Greasing soil-contacting parts after work minimizes corrosion; the draught of a rusty plough is much higher than for a shiny one.

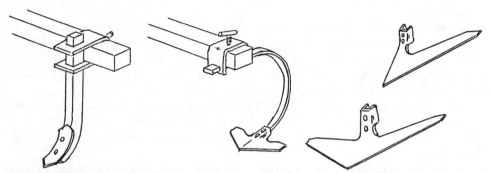

Tines and points (from left to right): rigid tine with chisel point; spring tine with duckfoot point; half and full sweeps for use with rigid tine.

Animal-powered intercultivation

Animal-powered intercultivation equipment may be classified as:
○ special-purpose intercultivation implements;
○ multi-purpose toolbars with a single small wheel for control and transport;
○ multi-purpose toolbars with two supporting wheels or skids.

Each type of implement is usually available with either rigid or spring tines to which may be fitted a variety of points, sweeps or mouldboards as shown above. Chisel points (about 3 or 4cm wide) and duck-foot points (10cm to 15cm) are usually fitted to spring tines whose vibration assists in bringing weeds to the surface and breaking down soil clods as well as reducing the risk of damage if an obstruction is met. Sweeps (up to 50cm wide) and left- or right-hand half-sweeps must be fitted to rigid tines. They are intended to work a few centimetres under the soil surface detaching weeds at the roots and leaving the dried-up remains on the surface where they may act as a mulch to reduce evaporation and improve erosion resistance of the soil. Mouldboard ridging bodies may be used in weeding and restoring ridges for ridge-grown crops.

The straddle-cultivator which is listed in this guide is a special-purpose machine which may be used for intercultivation. It has the particular advantage that it may be used to cultivate the sides of ridges as well as being suitable for work on the flat.

Multi-purpose toolbars with a single small wheel or skid generally cost less than special-purpose implements since the main toolbar frame is used, with various attachments for primary cultivation, seed-bed preparation, intercultivation and, possibly, planting. The width of the main frame may sometimes be varied by bolt-on extensions to deal with a range of row-crop spacings.

Multi-purpose animal-drawn toolbars are listed from p.29 of the guide.

Multi-purpose toolbars with two supporting wheels are the most expensive of the forms of animal-drawn implements. They generally have two large wheels, a ride-on seat for the operator and a 'lift' mechanism (hand- or foot-operated) to raise and lower the tines or other attachments when in use. The wheels are usually set at a track width of 1m to 1.5m to suit the rowcrop spacing. When intercultivating the toolbar must generally pass over at least one row of the growing crop so that a good clearance height is necessary under the frame to which the tines are attached. This frame may sometimes be movable from side to side to act as a 'steerage-hoe' under the control of an operator, making it easier to work close to the crop rows even if they have not been planted accurately in straight lines. Multi-purpose toolbars of this type are often used in conjunction with bed systems of cultivation.

Motorized Cultivation

For rain-fed crop production, motorized cultivators can be an asset to small farmers in areas where high-value crops are being grown and where fuel and service can be guaranteed. They are manufactured as two main types:

○ Single-axis, driving a rotivator without land wheels. For very light duties traction wheels can be fitted instead of the rotor, to pull draught implements.

○ Double axis, one driving traction wheels and one driving a rotivator. Being heavier and more powerful than the single-axle type the rotor can be removed and draught implements operated more effectively. Reversible mouldboard ploughs are often fitted to maximize field efficiency.

Alternatives

Although this section is concerned with tillage equipment, mention should be made of minimum tillage techniques, since these offer the most rapid method of crop establishment. Weeds are cut by shallow cultivation and they form a mulch with crop residues from the previous season, through which seeds are planted. The mulch eventually breaks down and helps to maintain the soil's organic matter, so that the productive life of land can be extended without the need of a fallow period. Mulch on the surface of uncultivated soil also reduces the incidence of soil erosion.

WEEDING HOES

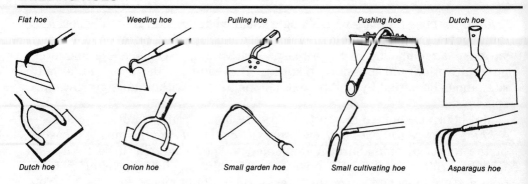

Flat hoe   Weeding hoe   Pulling hoe   Pushing hoe   Dutch hoe

Dutch hoe   Onion hoe   Small garden hoe   Small cultivating hoe   Asparagus hoe

Manufacturer	🔨	🔨	🔨	🔨	🔨	🖐	🔨	⌒	🔨	🔨	Other
Boral Cyclone Ltd, Australia		•					•		•	•	•
Bulldog Tools, United Kingdom			•	•		•				•	
Leon Clement & Cie, France	•	•	•	•	•	•			•	•	•
Cosmo Incorporated, Japan	•	•								•	
Cossul & Co. Pvt. Ltd, India											•
Edelmiro Vazquez Hno, Spain											
Elkem A/S, Norway		•					•		•		•
Korea Trade Promotion Corp, Korea		•								•	
Kumaon Nursery, India										•	
Manufacture Française de Fourches, France		•	•	•	•	•	•	•	•	•	•
Outils Wolf, France	•						•		•	•	•
Polar Werke GmbH, West Germany			•	•			•		•	•	•
Neill Tools Ltd, United Kingdom			•		•	•		•	•	•	
Wolf Tools for Garden & Lawn Ltd, UK	•						•		•	•	•

GLIDE-N-GROOM HOE

Goserud produce this hoe which is operated by a push and pull motion, cutting weeds below the surface. Blade 16cm wide. Similar models are produced by the other manufacturers listed below.

LEON CLEMENT, FRANCE
MANUFACTURE FRANÇAISE DE FOURCHES, FRANCE

TANGED PAXTON HOE

Bulldog produce the hoe in 2 sizes 152mm and 200mm width. The finish is half bright and is shaped on the two front faces. It is fitted with a 1.5m handle.

BULLDOG, U.K.
POLAR WERKE, W. GERMANY

TURNIP HOE

This hoe from Elkem Spigerverket is 70mm wide with a 137cm handle. It weighs 0.8kg.

ELKEM SPIGERVERKET, NORWAY

SPINTILLER

This 'revolutionary' implement's pairs of blades are set at about 12° to the vertical so that they converge in a slide-slicing and rotary chopping motion which cuts into the ground in a digging, pinching action. A 2-tine head is also available.

BULLDOG, U.K.
OUTILS WOLF, FRANCE
WOLF, U.K.

CHAVROT EMANCHE

Léon Clément produce this swan-necked hoe in two sizes weighing 1000g, for the small model, and 1100g for the large model.

LEON CLEMENT, FRANCE

METZ NANCY

Léon Clément produce this forged swan-necked hoe. It is available in 3 widths (of 3 differing weights) 140mm (0.4kg), 160mm (0.5kg), 180mm (0.6kg). Also available is the broader, 260mm (0.8kg) 'Chapeau de Gendarme' hoe, a broad blade with a raised, rounded centre to which the neck is attached.

LEON CLEMENT, FRANCE

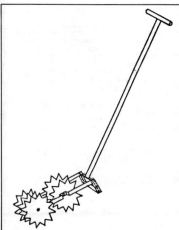

STAR WEEDER

The star weeder is used for the intercultivation of row crops such as vegetables, groundnuts, jowar etc. It is only suitable for dryland farming. The star-shaped cutting edges chop weeds and rake the topsoil, creating good mulching conditions. There are three blades at the front, and two at the rear. This implement can cover 0.2ha per day, and according to the manufacturers, is almost 50 per cent more cost-efficient for weeding than the hand kurpi. The star weeder can also be worked across the rows to contribute to earthing operations.

ANDHRA PRADESH AGRICULTURAL UNIVERSITY
Rajendranagar
Hyderabad 500 030
INDIA

SHARMA HAND HOE

This hoe manufactured in 3 widths by Cossul has 3 cutting edges. Suitable for heavily weed-infested plots. Capacity is about 0.05 ha/h.

COSSUL, INDIA

PUSH-AND-PULL HOE

Cyclone produce this hoe used for cutting weeds below the soil surface. The blade width is 175mm and the handle is 1330mm long.

The standard pack for all of Cyclone's hoes (and also their mattocks and picks) contains six implements.

BORAL CYCLONE, AUSTRALIA

MULTIHOE

The Multihoe is a cleverly designed new tool which can perform many soil-moving tasks in vegetable gardens. Additionally it has a lock recess on its upper edge which enables it to cut thicker weed stems. Among the tasks it can perform are:
HOEING Draw it backwards and forwards to use the bottom cutting edge and point.
WEEDING Use the lock recess to cut plant stalks.
EARTHING & TRENCHING Use the Multihoe's plough shape to create a smooth rounded trench, or for earthing-up.
SEEDING & PLANTING Draw the hoe through the soil to create a seed drill, or lift and strike the point down to make deep holes for planting.
Available in 5 sizes with short (15cm) or long handles.

MULTIHOE GARDEN TOOLS
Hayne Barton
Stowford, Lewdown
Devon EX20 4BZ
U.K.

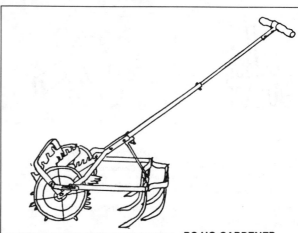

RO-HO GARDENER

Push the hoe and the sawtooth blades bite into the soil and leave a pulverized mulch. The sharpened scuffle blade cuts off the weeds, and permits work close to the plants even when small. Reverse the hoe and it is ready for deep cultivation. The hoe is completely adjustable. Not recommended for stony or trashy soil.

Various models in sizes up to 35cm wide available from:

AMERICAN LAWN MOWER CO.
P.O. Box 369
Shelbyville, IN 46176
U.S.A.

MAHARASHTRA AGRO IND. DEV. CORPORATION LTD.
Rajan House, 3rd Floor
Near Century Bazar, Prabhadevi
Bombay 400 025
INDIA

HAND-PUSHED CULTIVATOR

This is a very versatile multipurpose toolbar type of hoe. The frame is of metal. It has an overall length of 1.52m and a chassis width of 0.30m, and the handle is held 0.61-0.91m above the ground. It has a weight of 6.4kg. It can be used with one wheel (for cultivating between crop rows) or two wheels (for cultivating both sides of a single crop row).

The following attachments are available: a 20cm V-shaped skimmer for hoeing in soil with no stones; pulverising star-shaped rotating blades for breaking up soil; rakes for seed-bed preparation; 'duckfoot' cultivators for aeration and prevention of weeds; and a ridger for root crops.

JALO ENGINEERING LTD.
Wimborne Industrial Estate
Mill Lane, Wimborne
Dorset
U.K.

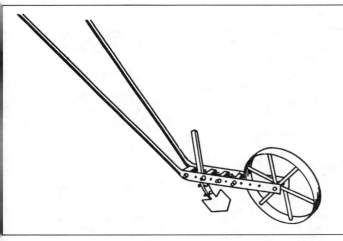

HAND WHEEL HOE

This implement consists of a wheel, a frame and a hoe. It works on the same principle as the Tropic and Union Forgings hoes described above. The major difference however, is the V-shaped tine which cuts the weeds and, at the same time, moves earth to right and left to form small ridges on either side of it. Thus it also performs an earthing operation. The hoe is 150mm wide and 150mm long. The fixed height of the whole implement is 950mm.

MAHARASHTRA AGRO IND. DEV. CORPORATION
Rajan House, 3rd Floor
Near Century Bazar, Prabhadevi
Bombay 400 025
INDIA

designed to be used even in the hardest ground. The wheel has bearings on both sides for durability. The cutting tools consist of 2 cutting blades, 19cm long, and a goosefoot plough, 10cm wide, which is adustable up, down and sideways. It is possible to fit an attachment for heaping up the soil.

TRÖSTER LANDMASCHINENFABRIK
GmbH & Co. Kg
P.O. Box 240, 6308 Butzbach
W. GERMANY

ONE WHEEL HOES

ONE WHEEL HOE — 'RADANA' Removal of weeds and loosening of soil crusts is achieved by this type of cutting blade (illustrated above). The wheel can be adjusted by means of screws in the forks for height and depth. The blade is

HIGH-HOE The High Hoe is strongly constructed yet light and easy to use. It has two horizontal blades which can be adjusted by simply undoing two wing-nuts, and placing them in numerous different positions for either centre or side hoeing. The handles can be adjusted to 3 different heights for ease of use.

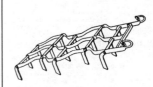

FLEXIBLE HARROW

Each row of 3 tines is able to move independently. The harrow has a working width of 0.6m, a length of 1.3m and weighs 21kg.

DOV YODLA & SONS
P.O. Box 246, Givatayim 53102
ISRAEL

HAND WHEEL-HOES

The hand wheel-hoes manufactured by Union Forgings and Tropic (illustrated left) are designed for the efficient intercultivation of row crops by one operator. Weeds are cut by the action of the rear-mounted blade passing through the soil. The operator pushes and pulls this blade whilst standing in one place, before moving along the row. They are easy to operate and require little effort. The Union Forgings model differs in having right-angle bent handles instead of D-shaped handles, and a V-shaped blade.

UNION FORGINGS
Focal Point
Sherpur, Ludhiana
Punjab
INDIA

TROPIC
B.P. 706, Douala
CAMEROUN

SQUARE HARROW

The frame of the square harrow is two T-sections. It has 21 threaded teeth and a levelling board.

RUMPSTAD B.V.
3243 ZG Stad Aan't-Haringvliet
Postbus 1
NETHERLANDS

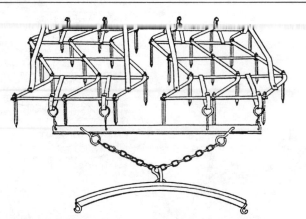

ZIGZAG HARROWS

So called because of the zigzag formation of the framework, these harrows are equipped with fixed vertical tines and are manufactured in a wide range of weights and sizes. The lightest type, which may have a track of up to 5m, is used for covering over broadcast seeds, and has relatively short tines. The heavier animal-drawn zigzag harrows have a narrower track and larger tines for better penetration in hard soil conditions.

Zigzag harrows are usually used in 'gangs' where the desired track width is made up with one or more harrow units. For animal-drawn implements, the maximum number of gangs is normally 4, depending on the weight of the harrow and the draught power available.

For transportation purposes, zigzag harrows are fitted with metal skids on the upper side of the framework.

The following manufacturers produce 2-, 3- or 4-gang, 16-tooth harrows (4 rows of 4 teeth). They are available in three sizes — light, medium and heavy — with gang weights ranging from 26 to 40kg. Teeth are 200-225mm in length with a 30 × 12mm section.

ETS. TÉCHINÉ,
82400 Valence d'Agen (T&G)
FRANCE

S.C.A.D. BOURGUIGNON,
B.P. 17, 26301 Bourg-de-Péage-Cedex

Drome
FRANCE

MARPEX
1 rue Thurot, 44000 Nantes
FRANCE

RAU MASCHINENFABRIK GmbH
Johannes-Rau-Straße
7315 Weilheim an der Teck
W. GERMANY

SPRING-TINED CULTIVATORS

Similar in function to the spring-tooth harrows, these cultivators are designed to be drawn by a pair of horses or oxen.

U-407/0 SPRING-TINE CULTIVATOR
It has 5 replaceable spring tines, each with a doubled-edged point. The working depth of the tines can be set by a control lever. This raises or lowers a frame to which the tines are attached.
Specifications include:
working depth: up to 15cm.
working width: 75cm.
average output: 0.25 ha/h
total weight: 85kg.
This cultivator is manufactured by Wytwornia Urzadzeń Komunalnych of Kalisz and is available through:

AGROMET MOTOIMPORT
Foreign Trade Enterprise
P.O. Box 990
Warsaw
POLAND

HORSE-DRAWN CULTIVATOR
This cultivator is manufactured with 9 or 11 tines with respective working widths and weights of 80cm/140kg and 120cm/160kg. Depth of cultivation is regulated by a shift lever which is coupled to all 4 wheels. This allows the support frame always to be parallel to the ground.

K.K. LIEN FABRIKK A/S
Tromøy, Arendal
4812 Kongshamn
NORWAY

SC12 CULTIVATOR

Also available is the SC12 horse-drawn cultivator with spring tines adaptable for 2- or 3-horse draught:

CARTHORSE CO. LTD.
Egremont Farm, Payhembury
Honiton, Devon EX14 0JA
U.K.

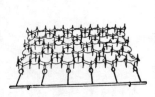

CHAIN HARROW

The chain harrow comprises up to 5 rows of interlinking 'tridents' (3 spiked teeth mounted on a steel ring). Two working widths of 1.5 and 1.75m are available with weights ranging from 32 to 77kg.

NARDI FRANCESCO & FIGLI
06017 Selci Lama, Perugia
ITALY

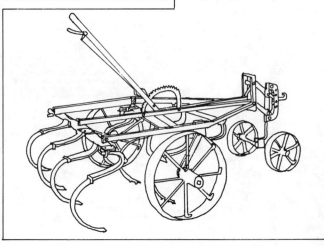

THE ADAPTABAR

A heavy-duty, multi-purpose toolbar strong enough to be used with a 2 or 4 oxen team or pulled by a small tractor. Additional attachments to the 3- or 5-tine cultivator, 22 cm plough and planet ridger pictured here include: roller seeder, groundnut/potato lifter, two-row planter, subsoiler, 5-tine sweep and roller clod breaker. These may be combined where appropriate.

Attachments are retained by ring bolts passing through the stalk, but the thrust is taken by the central frame inserts which are welded in place. Twin A-shaped tube handles can also be supplied.

A heavier frame for hard soil conditions is also available.

PROJECT EQUIPMENT LTD.
Industrial Estate, Rednal Airfield
West Felton, Oswestry
Salop SY11 4HS
U.K.

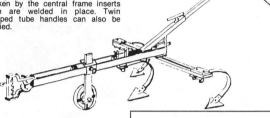

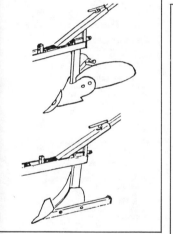

HAND RIDGERS

Hand ridgers are employed in manual land forming and intercultivation operations. When attached to a handle-bar they can be pulled through the soil to form ridges.

HAND RIDGER

MANUFACTURE FRANCAISE DE FOURCHES
3 rue de Lyon, Terrenoire, B.P. 4
42011 Saint-Etienne Cedex
FRANCE

HEAPER
The 'heaper' is available in 2 sizes. The No.3H5 is 20cm wide, while the 3H6 model has a width of 26cm.

POLAR WERKE GmbH
Postfach 14 04 60
5630 Remscheid 1
W. GERMANY

RIDGER
This is a tool for ridging, earthing up vegetables, trenching etc., and can be pulled through the soil at walking pace.

WOLF TOOLS LTD.
Ross-on-Wye, Herefordshire HR9 5NE
U.K.

EARTHING PLOUGH
This is a hand-drawn tool with a seamless steel blade for planting and earthing over potatoes, tracing irrigation channels etc.

HAND-DRAWN PLOUGH
When fitted with a guiding and pulling handle, this plough makes an excellent tool for planting and harvesting potatoes, and can be operated by two people.

POLYNOL ANIMAL-DRAWN AGRICULTURAL TOOL BAR

The Polynol is the most sophisticated of the Belin range of animal-drawn toolbars. For the three chassis types produced for this model, the following attachments are available:
- plough (1 or 2 bodies)
- reversible plough
- cultivator
- harrow
- disc harrow
- sub-soiler
- ridger
- lifter
- ridge leveller
- leveller
- cereal seeder
- fertilizer spreader
- precision seeder
- sprayer
- ridge seeder
- furrow seeder
- grass cutter
- rotary reaper
- charrette
- tip cart
- water tank
- unloading cart
- semi-trailer
- weeder
- hoe
- mixer
- roller
- ridge with disc
- cane-sugar planter
- potato planter

BELIN INTERNATIONAL
2 Mail des Charmilles
B.P. 194, 10006 Troyes Cedex
FRANCE

THE NIKART is available from:

GEEST OVERSEAS
MECHANISATION LTD,
Marsh Lane, Boston
Lincolnshire PE21 7RP, UK

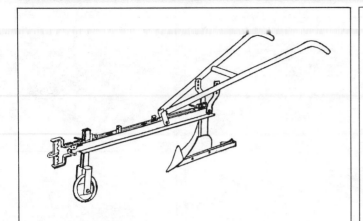

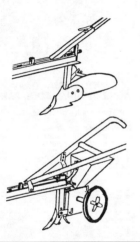

THE ANGLEBAR

Considerably lighter than the Adaptabar, the Anglebar is a multi-purpose model which is within the pulling capacity of smaller draught animals such as ponies, mules, or small oxen.

Available attachments shown are the 22 cm plough, planet ridger and roller seeder.

The Anglebar is manufactured from steel sections which are widely available in many countries, and is intended for production in small workshops possessing only basic equipment.

The main frame is made from angle iron, with handles of water pipe (either A- or T-shaped). The handles are adjustable for height, and the attachments are secured by ring bolts passing through the stalk and mounting points on the frame.

PROJECT EQUIPMENT LTD.
Industrial Estate, Rednal Airfield
West Felton, Oswestry
Salop SY11 4HS
U.K.

ROLLERS

After ploughing, uneven ground can be levelled to some extent by the use of a roller. Rolling is also practised as a secondary tillage operation, to break down clods and consolidate seedbeds.

HAND-PUSHED ROLLER
The illustration shows this roller by Al-Ko. It has a single cyclinder and is designed to be pushed by one person.

AL-KO BRITAIN LTD.
No.1 Industrial Estate
Medomsley Road, Consett
County Durham DH8 6SZ
U.K.

ANIMAL OR TRACTOR-DRAWN
ROLLER
A large roller consisting of two cylinders, each with a diameter of 0.6m, a draw-bar and a seat.

It is available in two widths. The smaller size is 1.6m wide and weighs 223kg and the larger model is 2m wide and weighs 250kg.

ETS. TÉCHINÉ
82400 Valence d'Agen (T & G)
FRANCE

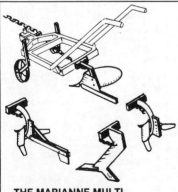

THE MARIANNE MULTI-PURPOSE TOOL BAR

MARIANNE is the third in Belin's range of multi-purpose cultivators, and offers more sophisticated characteristics than the Simone and Kanol. Drawn by 1 or 2 animals, instead of a single-bar frame, the 'Marianne' features a rectangular frame onto which 1 to 3 wheels and one of a choice of 12 implements may be attached. Being larger than the other models it is able to handle double-row attachments and cultivators with a higher capacity than those with 3 tines only.

Available attachments are:
1. Single plough
2. Reverse plough
3. Cultivator (7-tine)
4. Furrower
5. Ridger
6. Peanut lifter
7. Double plough
8. Cultivator (5-tine)
9. Canadian harrow
10. Potato lifter
11. Subsoiler
12. Seeder

BELIN INTERNATIONAL
2 Mail des Charmilles, B.P. 194
10006 Troyes Cedex
FRANCE

WALKING TRACTOR 306

The special feature of this tractor is the 'quickfit' coupling for attachments which allows rapid change between a wide range of accessories powered through the PTO.

Technical specifications:
Engine type: Petrol 9-10 hp or Diesel 8 hp.

Gears: 4 speed: 3 forward, 1 reverse.
Tilling width: 26-65cm.

BERTOLINI MACCHINE AGRICOLE,
SpA
42100 Reggio Emilia
Via Guicciardi
ITALY

HEAVY-DUTY MULTIPURPOSE TILLERS

These heavy-duty tillers are designed to perform a wide range of tasks. They have two large tyred wheels and a variety of accessories which can be fitted for ploughing, weeding, mowing, transporting etc. Most of the manufacturers listed here and in the lightweight cultivation table on the previous page produce a range of heavy duty cultivators. A few are listed on this page.

TIGER
Technical Specifications:
  Engine type: Diesel.
  Power output: 10hp.
  Gears: 9 speeds: 3 forward and 1 reverse in both running directions and 1 for road circulation.
  Power take-off: Two; one of which is synchronized with all gears.
  Attachments: Rotavator, trailer, plough, spray and irrigation pump, mower etc.
  Four other models are available.

BARBIERI SpA
Via Circonvallazione, 19
36040 Sossano, Vicenza
ITALY

MODEL 2400
This model (illustrated on the left) has the following technical specifications:
  Engine type: Diesel.
  Power Output: 9hp.
  Gears: 6 speeds: 3 forward, 3 reverse.
  Power take-off: Independent.
  Weight: 85kg (without attachments).
  Tillage width: 5 widths: 32-65cm.
  Attachments: Rotavators, ploughs, cutter bars, ridger, cultivator, harrow, trailer.
  7 and 8hp models are also available.

AGRIA WERKE GmbH
Postfach 1147
7108 Möckmühl
W. GERMANY

F800 ROTARY TILLER
The F800 is a tiller with a high power-to-weight ratio. It has adjustable handle bars and can be used with or without wheels. The wheel tracks are adjustable to suit varying row widths.
  Technical Specifications:
  Engine type: Petrol.
  Power output: 7hp maximum.
  Gears: 8 speeds: 6 forward, 2 reverse.
  Power take-off: 2.
  Dry weight: 110kg.
  Tilling width: Up to 95cm.
  Attachments: Slasher rotor, drum rotor, plough, weeder, ridger, dozer, 5-tine tool bar.
  A 5hp model, the HONDA F600, is also available.

HONDA (U.K.) LTD.
Power Road, London W4 5YT
U.K.

Technical characteristics of typical light-weight cultivators

Manufacturer	Country	Model	2 or 4 stroke	Power output (or displacement)	Gears	Power take off	Weight (kg)	Maximum or range of working width (cm)	Traction wheels	Coulter discs	Rotavator	Ridger	Weeder	Trailer
Agria Werke	W. Germany	100-4	4	4hp	1	No	49	45-77	●		●			
Al-Ko	U.K.	Farmer 300 B	2	3hp	1	No	26	60			●			
Barbieri	Italy	Minizappa	2	4hp	2	No	42		●		●			●
Courmont	France	SAM	4	(161cc)	1	No		34-62		●	●	●	●	
Danarm	U.K.	TV 3	4	3	1	Yes			●	●	●	●	●	●
Ferrari	Italy	32 E	2	5hp	1	No	55	30-70	●		●			
Granja	France	GB 412	4	(127cc)	1	No		60			●			
Gutbrod Werke	W. Germany	MB 66-50	4	4.5hp	1	No					●			
Honda (U.K.)	U.K.	F400	4	3.5hp	6	Yes	45.5	95	●	●	●	●	●	●
Howard														
Alatpertanian	Malaysia	Stinger	2	3.5hp	1	No		61	●		●			●
Kanematsu-Gosho	Japan	MR7 4T	2	3.3hp	1	No	32	66.5	●		●	●		
M.A.B.	Italy	Formica 2T/4	2	4hp	1	Yes	50	40-60			●			●
Mason & Porter	New Zealand	Rotahoe	4	5hp	2	No	58	61			●			
Mechgard	U.K.	Terratiller	4		1	No			●		●	●	●	
Motostandard	France	MST60-32	4	(127cc)	2	No		60			●			
Ohashi	Japan	AR-551-651				Yes					●			
P.G.S.	Italy	MZ 503-505	2		1	No		40-80		●	●			
Charles Pugh	U.K.	Atco	4	3hp	2	No	50	60		●	●		●	
G.E.P.	Italy	S.E.P. 35	4	3.5hp	2	Yes	64	55-70	●	●	●	●	●	
Staub	France	ST 300	4	(148cc)	1	No	38	53		●	●	●	●	
Szegedi	Hungary	RK 02	4		1	No		34-60		●	●			
Wolseley Webb	U.K.	Super Major	4	3.5	2	No	44	94	●	●	●	●	●	

3. Sowing, planting, and fertilizer distribution

In order to achieve good yields when growing vegetables, cereals, legumes and root crops, the depth of seeding and the spacing between the plants should be uniform and optimal for the given growing conditions. However, to facilitate weeding and other operations the plants are often confined to rows, usually with a distance between them that is less than that between the rows. To achieve the best compromise, various designs of hand-operated and animal-drawn seeders and planters have been developed which control, to a greater or lesser extent, the plant density by means of the spacing in each row of seeds and other planting material. Most seeders and planters can also be used to distribute fertilizer. Combined seeder/fertilizer drills are used to drill fertilizer into the soil at the optimal distance from the seeds at the same time as sowing.

Seeders and fertilizers

Seeds and planting material are placed in the ground in three ways:
○ Seeds can be broadcast on the soil and are then usually buried by raking, harrowing or scattering earth over them.
○ Seeds, tubers or other vegetative material, and seedlings can be placed in holes in the ground which are then refilled with soil.
○ Seeds and other planting material can be placed in a furrow, opened to the appropriate depth, then closed again and lightly compressed.

Broadcasting

Broadcasting can be done by hand scattering or by using a hand-operated broadcaster which is usually slung over the shoulder of the operator. These broadcasters are often called seed fiddles, a name acquired because of the bow stick handle used to drive the spinner. The leather thong of the bow passes around a bobbin which is attached to the ribbed spinner. By moving the bow from left to right the spinner rotates, scattering the seed which falls onto it from the canvas seed bag. The rate of seedling can be altered by loosening a wing-nut under the fiddle and moving the slide to the setting required, thus altering the aperture of the hole through which the seed trickles. Broadcasting requires considerable skill on the part of the operator to achieve an even distribution.

Alternatively a uniform coverage can be achieved by a spinning-disc distributor driven by its wheels through a gear box. These are usually two-wheeled and can be pulled or pushed by one person, with larger versions being animal-drawn.

Dibbling

Dibbling seeds and other planting material in holes in the soil is the oldest form of planting. Distances between plants can be precisely determined by the operator. Often more than one seed or plant is placed in each hole. A variety of pointed sticks, some with metal tips, are commonly used for this purpose. Manually operated 'walking stick' and rotary injection 'jab' planters are used for both seeds and fertilizers. Jab planters can be used in quite rough seed beds or uncultivated land, so long as the land is soft enough. They are useful for filling gaps in rows and can also be used to place fertilizers.

The principle of 'jab-planting', as applied to the rotary injection machine, incorporates six jabbing devices around its circumference. Hand-pushed versions of this design have been developed and introduced in Nigeria with some success.

Seed is picked up from the hopper by the feed roller which contains pockets of a suitable size for the crop concerned. The seeds then fall into the jabbing devices which remain closed until just before withdrawal from the soil, at which point they open and the seeds drop into the hole. The distance between each jab depends on the diameter of the rotary wheel, the length of the jabbing devices and the depth to which the jabbing devices penetrate the soil; for maize the distance between holes is about 250mm. This is achieved by a wheel of about 350mm in diameter with the jabbing devices protruding by about 75mm.

A variation of the dibbler is used to plant large vegetative material (e.g. potatoes), seedlings, or cuttings. The soil engaging point of the planter can be opened wide enough to allow the material to be placed manually at the correct depth.

Row seeding

Row seeding or planting can, at its simplest, be achieved with a plough or other furrow-making tool and the seeds or other material are dropped in the furrow at the appropriate intervals. The furrow can then be closed. Hand-pushed row seeders (usually single row) normally require a well-prepared seed-bed. In unmetered seeders the seed usually trickles into the furrow from a mounted container. Alternatively, in animal-drawn one- and two-row seeders an operator is sometimes required to feed the material manually, either by means of a sowing tube or directly into the furrow.

Fertilizer distributors

The distribution of manure and fertilizer is often done entirely by hand. Organic manures and composts are usually spread over a whole field or between plant rows and incorporated by subsequent cultivation. Similarly, inorganic fertilizers can be broadcast by hand scattering or by using mechanical broadcasters. They can also be placed on the surface between plant rows and then be incorporated, or be dibbled in beside plants or seed placements. Granular or pelleted fertilizer can be drilled into the soil at an appropriate distance from the plants using seeders. This method of distribution is often done at the same time as seeding or planting, frequently using dual-purpose equipment.

Advantages

The benefits of using precision equipment are higher crop yields. These should be achieved because:
○ Correct seeding depths lead to better germination and uniform crop stands.
○ Precision seeding results in an optimum plant population and reduces seed consumption.
○ Good quality seeders improve the speed and accurate timing of the sowing.
○ Use of row seeders/planters allows easier weeding and other operations; it also makes possible contour planting which may help to reduce erosion.
○ Fertilizer drilled into the soil provides plants with readily available nutrients; the timing of application can be related to the plants' needs.

Alternatives

The more labour-intensive methods referred to above have been used since agriculture began. They are still the commonest methods used by poor smallholders. Although precision equipment is not used, the quality of planting need not be any less optimal, given sufficient care and the time of skilled operators. And in certain circumstances — e.g. when sowing stony uncultivated land, or when using odd corners of fields or in gardens — these labour-intensive methods are the only viable ones.

SEEDERS

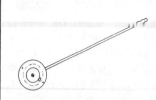

PLANT-RITE ROW SEEDER

Earthway produced this hand-pushed garden seeder with the domestic market in mind, but it may have a wider application. Ideal for vegetable seeding it is light (1½ kg) and has a calibration dial which covers all common vegetable seed types.

EARTHWAY PRODUCTS INC.
P.O. Box 547
Maple Street, Bristol, IN 46507
U.S.A.

SEED SOWER

This instrument is similar to the Earthway model except that it can be used to plant a wider variety of seeds up to the size of a small pea.

WOLF TOOLS FOR GARDEN & LAWN LTD
Ross-on-Wye
Herefordshire HR9 5NE
U.K.

OUTILS WOLF
Rue de l'Industrie, 67160 Wissembourg
FRANCE

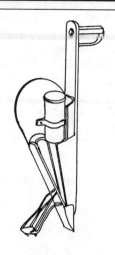

HAND MAIZE PLANTER

This simple spring-action jab planter places single seeds at the required depth. The planter is placed in the ground at a certain depth and pushed forward onto the spring-loaded foot. This action causes the point to open and deposit a seed in the soil. At the same time the seeder is recharged from the hopper. A spring action mechanism returns the planter to the vertical and the operator then removes the planter from the soil (usually) walking backwards to plant the next seed. Interchangeable discs with variable hole sizes can be used for planting single seeds for a range of crops from millet to beans. It is particularly useful for planting cotton, maize and groundnuts.

COSSUL & CO. PVT. LTD.
123/367 — Industrial Area
Fazalgunj, Kanpur, U.P.
INDIA

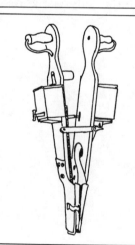

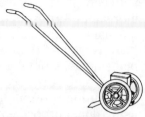

EXEL HAND SEEDER

Designed for most types of vegetable seed, this hand-pushed seeder is suitable for small areas of well-prepared land. The two rubber-tyred wheels drive the seeding mechanism which is supplied by a one-litre capacity hopper.

RUSSELLS (KIRBYMOORSIDE) LTD.
Kirbymoorside
Yorkshire YO6 6DJ
U.K.

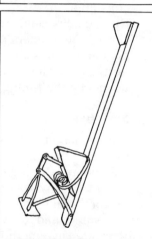

HAND SEEDERS

Better Farming Equipment supply 2 models, one with a hopper and one without. For the latter the seed is hand-fed down a tube in the handle when the point is open in the soil. This is a valuable method for filling in gaps in rows. (Illustration above.)

B.F. EQUIPMENT
30080 Sde Yaakov
ISRAEL

COMBINED FERTILIZER AND SEED PLANTER

This instrument is suitable for a variety of seed crops. The double-action mechanism can be adjusted to allow the required flow of seed and fertilizer. Several other models are available. (Illustration left.)

KRUPP
Schier and Cia Ltda
Rua Bento Gonçalves 3030
93,300 Novo Hamburgo, RS
BRAZIL

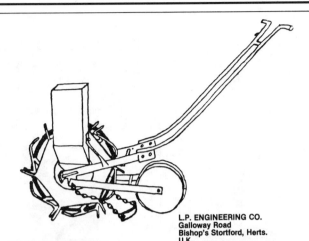

ROTARY INJECTION PLANTERS

Rotary injection planters are similar to jab planters. The seed or grain is held in a hopper and introduced into the soil by six punches mounted on a rotating planting wheel. The instruments described here are all manually operated with weights of around 25 kg, and are suitable for a variety of seeds and grains. The seeds are planted at the required depth with spacings determined by adjustments which can be made to the instrument. The performance of rotary injection planters varies according to seed type and nature of terrain, but a rate of ⅛ ha per hour for maize, for example, can be expected.

An advantage of rotary injection planters is the wide range of conditions in which they can be used, even when the soil is uncultivated and terrain rough. These planters can be recommended when minimal tillage is being practised and/or when efforts are being made to reduce soil erosion by planting rougher seed beds.

L.P. ENGINEERING CO.
Galloway Road
Bishop's Stortford, Herts.
U.K.

POYING'S WELDING SHOP
262 National Hi-Way
Brgy, Anos, Los Banos, Laguna
PHILIPPINES

NDUME PRODUCTS LTD.
P.O. Box 62, Gilgil
KENYA

GEEST OVERSEAS MECHANISATION LTD.
Marsh Lane, Boston
Lincolnshire PE21 7RP
U.K.

MAHINDRA ENTERPRISES
507 Prince of Wales Avenue
Colombo 14
SRI LANKA

MBP ENGINEERING
KM 16 MacArthur Highway
Malanday, Valenzuela
Metro Manila
PHILIPPINES

ELA AGRIC. MACHINERY MFG. AND ENGINEERING COMPANY
E9/914B Iwo Road, Ibadan
NIGERIA

SINGLE-ROW HAND SEEDERS

These hand seed drills are a little more advanced than a simple model such as the ASPEE APS-54. Although very similar in operation, having furrow openers, coverers, press and ground wheels, these seeders are equipped with inter-changeable seed plates. The seed plates allow for adjustments to be made for a wide range of seed types. The actual seeding process is gravity fed from a mounted hopper from which the seeds are released by an agitator sprocket.

These models feature row markers and seed cut-offs, and weigh between 15-19 kg.

The Cossul model is illustrated above (top illustration).

The Tröster model is illustrated above (lower illustration). Manufacturers of similar machines are also listed below.

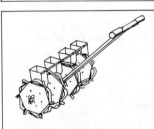

TECHNOHAC AGRICULTURAL MACHINERY & IMPLEMENTS LTD.
New Industry Region
Petakh-Tikva, P.O.B. 225
ISRAEL

A.J. TRÖSTER
LANDMASCHINENFABRIK Gmbh & CO. KG
P.O. Box 240
6408 Butzbach
W. GERMANY

MULTI-PURPOSE PRECISION SEEDER

EBRA produce 2 hand seeders (Type XJ1 and Type XJ2) suitable for market gardens or smallholdings. They can be used for almost any seed or grain type.

The XJ1 model, shown here, can sow singly in lines or in multi-seed hills. It has 2 distributors for small and medium seeds, and a chain-driven seeding mechanism with changeable chain wheels for different seed spacings. The seed hopper has a 5-litre capacity and the furrowing blade can be adjusted to the required planting depth. The XJ1 is also fitted with adjustable covering blades and a weighted roller. In addition this seeder can be supplied with other seed distributors and a row marker extendable to 60cm. There is also a XJ2 model with a disconnector for the seed distributor.
E.B.R.A.
28 Rue du Maine
B.P. 915, 49009 Angers Cedex, France

4-ROW PLANTER

The hand-pulled planter is intended for upland rice and gives a seed spacing of 25 x 25 cm. It is recomended only for upland soils which can be drained during seeding to provide air for germination.

GEEST OVERSEAS MECHANISATION LTD.
Marsh Lane, Boston
Lincolnshire PE21 7RP
U.K.

MULTI-ROW SEEDERS

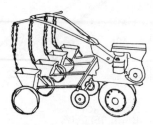

MULTI-UNIT PRECISION SEED DRILL

This all-steel seed drill can be used to plant any kind of seed.

The seeding mechanism is a brush running over a nylon cell wheel at the base of the hopper directly above an adjustable sowing coulter. Each cell wheel covers one grade seed size and requirements should be stated when ordering this machine. A useful feature of the machine is that it can be ordered in single hand-pushed units or any multiple of this depending on draught power available to the farmer.

ALVAN BLANCH DEVELOPMENT CO. LTD.
Chelworth
Malmesbury SN16 9SG, Wilts.
U.K.

PRECISION HAND-SEEDER AND FERTILIZER DRILL

Precision seeders can be used to plant a wide variety of vegetable seeds through six easily interchangeable seed plates which regulate the seed flow from the hopper to the planting mechanism. The seeder when in use opens the soil, plants the seeds at the desired spacing and depth, and covers the seeds while marking the adjacent row.

An additional and optional feature of this seeder is a fertilizer applicator for side dressing. It allows for a calibrated application of granulated fertilizers next to the seed row being planted at the required depth up to 5 cm.

EARTHWAY PRODUCTS INC.
P.O. Box 547
Maple Street, Bristol, IN 46507, U.S.A.

LAMBERT CORP.
P.O. Box 278
Ansonia
OH 45303

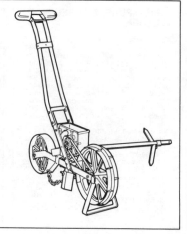

JAB PLANTER

Originally designed at the Asian Institute of Technology, Bangkok, this hand-operated planter can plant areas of soya bean and small seeds at a depth of 4 cm. The single action of jabbing the planter into the ground actuates the seeding mechanism and the seeds are deposited into the hole in the soil on the upward spring-assisted return stroke. The simple aluminium seeding drum can be cut out as required to give 2 different sized slots for the number of seeds per unit area, for 2 types of seed. A retracting foot pedal is featured for use in harder soil conditions.

CHAIPRADIT KARNCHANG
235 MOO 8
Chiang Mai-Hang Dong Road
A-Hang Dong, Chiang Mai
THAILAND

Also available is a very similar but slightly more sophisticated jab planter (not illustrated).

LAMBERT CORP.
P.O. Box 278
Ansonia
OH 45303, USA

RICMAR SEED FIDDLE

seed fiddle broadcast seeds and fertilizers. This model has 3 settings with the following performances:
1. 5.5 kg clover seed or 33 kg ryegrass seed per ha and 4.88 m at a cast; 2. 186 kg barley seed per ha and 7.32 m at a cast; 3. 278 kg oat seed per ha and 4.88 m at a cast.

M.E. TUDOR
Frogmore Cottage, Sawyers Mill, Minety
Nr. Maimesbury SN16 9QL, Wilts, U.K.

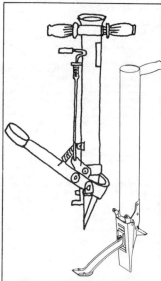

SPADE POTATO PLANTER

This instrument is designed for planting at the required depth. The planter is inserted into the ground and pushed forward to release the seed potato, the hole being covered with soil by the operator's foot. (Illustration above right.)

EARTHWAY PRODUCTS INC.
P.O. Box 547
Maple Street, Bristol, IN 46507
U.S.A.

TREE SEEDLING PLANTER

This hand-held seedling planter is used to transplant tree seedlings from the nursery bed directly into the ground at a permanent plantation site in such a way that the entire root system is covered by, and comes into contact with, the soil. (Illustration above left.)

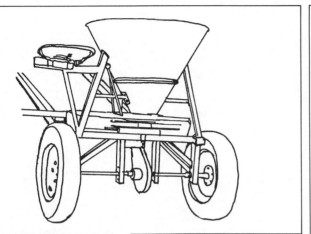

FERTILIZER SPREADER LS4

Designed to be pulled by any draught horse, the LS4 spreader can also be used by other animals such as mules and oxen. A strong box section steel chassis carries a rot-proof polythene hopper of 5 cwt capacity above an adjustable shutter operated by a lever beside the driver. Regulated by a simple pin and vernier system, the shutter aperture is variable to give different flow rates on to the spinner plate revolving below. Driven by a vee belt from a right-angle gearbox, the spinner is coupled by a chain and sprocket to the differential gear on the main axle. Both the gearbox and the differential box have sealed lubrication systems and require no maintenance. A feature of the LS4 is the incorporation of the differential which delivers a constant flow and therefore an even spread on any radius of corner while the hand lever gives instant cut-off on the headlands to avoid overspread.

THE CARTHORSE CO. LTD.
Egremont Farm, Payhembury
Honiton, Devon EX14 0JA
U.K.

GREEN MANURE BURYING TILLER MODEL MQ-51

This is powered by a 2-wheeled tractor and buries a 51 cm swathe of green crop up to 17 cm deep. The tiller pulverises the top soil, after burying the crop, making it ready without further tillage for cotton seeding. Manufactured by DONG THAI FARM EQUIPMENT, and available through:

CHINA NATIONAL AGRICULTURAL MACHINERY
Import and Export Corporation
26 South Yeutan Street, Beijing, CHINA

FLOWSOW SEED DRILL

The Flowsow Seed Drill is a novel instrument developed for the purpose of sowing seeds using a suspending fluid (gel) as a carrier instead of the more usual belts, chains, plates or cups. The main advantage of using the gel carrier as opposed to dry seeding is that all the seeds are planted in the same environment ensuring even emergence, and that the seeds will not be exposed to such wide moisture fluctuations in the soil. The use of a suspending fluid also permits the sowing of pre-germinated seeds.

The gel is simply prepared by mixing with water and leaving to stand for 20 minutes. The seeds are stirred in well, and then by taking a 5 ml sample, the average density of seeds can be calculated. As the drill delivers 5 ml of gel for every 135 mm of wheel travel (regardless of wheel speed), the required density of seeds in the gel can be achieved so that the seeds are then sown at the correct spacings.

The use of a liquid sowing medium enables even very small and irregularly shaped seeds to be distributed into the soil at the required spacing. Use of the gel also enables precise placement, close to the seeds, of additives such as pesticides, fungicides and fertilizers. These substances can be added to the gel at the seed-mixing stage and extruded together with the seeds.

The hopper has a capacity of 2.25 litres (sufficient gel to cover 100 m travelled by the drill) and the drill can sow seeds up to 8 mm in diameter. Overall weight is 10 kg.

FLOWSOW ENGINEERING CO.
Slides, Silverhill
Robertsbridge, Sussex TN32 5PA
U.K.

SEED FIDDLE

This shoulder-slung fiddle is suitable for broadcasting seeds, grain and granular fertilizers over small acreages or patches affected by flood or drought.
This model features 3 rate settings.

ALVAN BLANCH DEVELOPMENT CO. LTD.
Chelworth
Malmesbury SN16 9SG, Wilts.
U.K.

MASTER FERTILIZER SPREADER

This spreader is designed for use in small areas and is suitable for all kinds of fertilizer. It can be supplied either as a single-row unit, or, with an additional fitting, as a double row unit. Both can be operated by one person.

The spreader is operated by being pushed by hand and features a direct drive mechanism from the land wheel to the fertilizer metering wheel. The metering wheel is available in 3 sizes (22 mm, 18 mm and 14 mm), there being 2 wheels of each size. All wheels are interchangeable and can be used in any combination.

The spreader is made of mild steel and has a weight (empty) of 9.5 kg. The hopper has a capacity (granular fertilizer) of 12 kg.

L.P. ENGINEERING CO.
Galloway Road,
Bishop's Stortford, Herts.
U.K.

4. Harvesting and post-harvest crop processing

Harvesting and threshing

The crop-harvesting equipment available to smallholders has changed very little over the years. Knives, sickles and scythes continue to be the traditional tools used to harvest crops. There are some low-horsepower reapers, but because of their low field capacity, high cost and other problems, they are often not considered a suitable alternative to the manual methods. On the other hand, a large number of efficient, low-cost hand, foot or power-driven threshers have been developed for use on smallholdings.

The use of a sharp blade to cut the plant stem is the simplest form of removing a crop. In each culture a different form of blade has been devised for

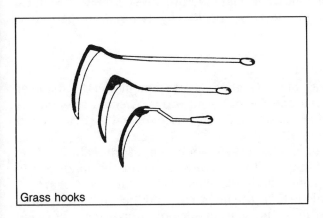

Grass hooks

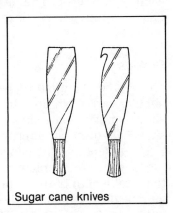

Sugar cane knives

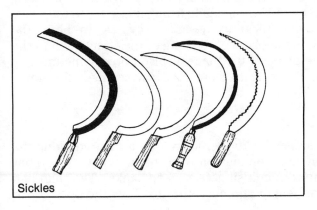

Sickles

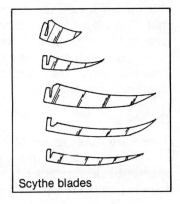

Scythe blades

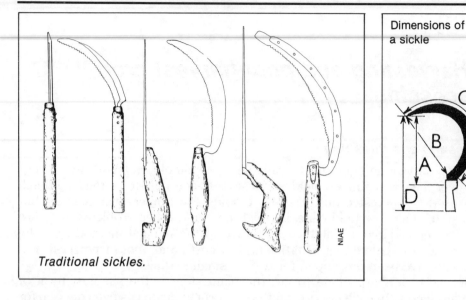

Dimensions of a sickle

Traditional sickles.

each type of crop. The most renowned manufacturer of scythes and sickles, Falci of Italy, have dozens of designs specifically tailored to particular markets.

Sickles

The degree of curvature, length of blade, angle of attachment and the shape of handle, vary from area to area and for different crops. A small selection is shown above. Some sickles have serrated edges but there is little evidence to show this to be an improvement.

The essential dimensions of sickles are shown in the diagram above. 'A' is the length of the implement, including the tang but excluding the handle. 'D' is the total length of the implement. The blade length is measured as the arc 'B' and the development of the blade 'C' is the length around the outer edge, up to but excluding the tang. The other measurement, not shown here, is blade thickness which is the greatest width of the blade from outer edge to the sharp edge. Similar measurements are used to describe scythes. In both, the curvature and distance between the plane of the tang or the attachment to the snath (scythe handle) and the plane of the blade, is also noted sometimes by manufacturers: the 'tang height measurement' and (in scythes) the 'tang-opening measurement'.

Scythes

These are long curved blades, usually 70 to 100cm long measured along the chord of the blade's arc (similar to dimension A in the drawing above), but shorter blades are available for difficult sites (e.g. steep banks). The shaft and handle (snath) designs vary in length and curvature to allow the operator to

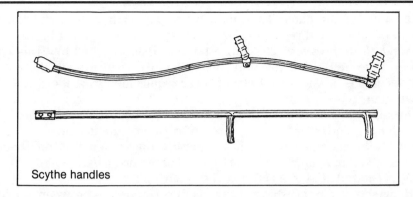

Scythe handles

work with outstretched arms and both hands at approximately the same height from the ground. Scythes can be fitted with a cradle attachment which collects the cut crop and allows it to be deposited at the end of the stroke.

Threshing equipment

Threshing equipment involves three quite distinct operations:
○ separating the grain from the panicle;
○ sorting the grain from the straw;
○ winnowing the chaff from the grain.
The first of these requires considerable energy and is the first to be mechanized. Sorting the grain from the straw is relatively easy but is the most difficult stage to mechanize. Winnowing is relatively easy, whether by machine or by hand.

Engine-powered threshing

Tractor-treading One method of threshing which has become widespread for wheat and barley is driving a tractor round and round on the crop spread over the threshing floor. If tyre pressure is kept low to minimize grain damage, excellent results are possible, and no added investment in machinery is required.

Hold-on threshers In areas where whole, undamaged straw is valued, some machines thresh rice by stripping grain from the panicles without damaging the straw. The simplest of these are mechanized versions of the treadle thresher in which the drum is rotated by a 1-3hp engine. Double-drum threshers contain two-wire looped cylinders. Most threshing is done in the slower, first cylinder which strips the grain on the panicles from the straw. The second, faster, cylinder is designed to thresh the broken panicles. Double-drum threshers are used for wheat and sorghum as well as paddy. Some have a self-feeding mechanism which continuously feeds the bundles into the machine, thus reducing the labour requirement.

Hold-on threshers require that the crop be formed up into even bundles, and this can be laborious if the crop was badly lodged or if even bundles were not harvested in the first place. Their main advantage is that they solve the major problem of all other threshers — how to separate the grain from the straw.

Through-flow threshers The entire harvested crop is fed into this type of thresher, thus increasing the bulk which has to pass through the machine. Faster feeding is possible but higher power requirements are inevitable. There are two main types:

— Tangential flow machines in which the crop passes directly through the threshing cylinder, around the circumference of the drum.
— Axial flow machines which have spirally positioned fins on the upper concave so that material fed in at one end of the drum passes along the drum as it is rotated, and is ejected at the other end.

In both machines the threshing occurs as the crop passes between a revolving cylinder and a metal grate called the concave, which covers part of the circumference of the drum. Threshed grain falls through the holes in the concave. The mechanism which causes the beating/rubbing which separates grain from straw and chaff can be of several types: wire loop, spike (or peg) tooth, rasp bar, angle bar.

Power for engine-driven threshers may be from a small engine mounted on the machine (2 or 3hp upwards), or from a tractor. Most machines allow adjustments for various crop and field conditions, and a large selection is available with varying drum, power supply and winnowing/cleaning arrangements. The simplest consist of little more than the threshing cylinder and concave mounted on a metal framework including feeding chute, outlets and a suitable engine.

More complex threshers which include winnowing fans and sieves to separate grain from straw and chaff include the axial-flow thresher developed by IRRI in the Philippines which has been widely adopted by rice producers. Also, the Alvan Blanch Minor thresher from the UK performs successfully with wheat, barley and sorghum; and various Indian-manufactured threshers are used primarily for wheat threshing. They are capable of very high outputs (0.5 to 2 or more tonnes per hour) and remove the need for hand winnowing, but are considerably more expensive and more difficult to repair in rural areas.

Separating grain from straw

The simplest way to separate grain from straw is to pick the straw up and shake it, letting the grain fall out. A better method is to use a pitchfork to do the shaking. The earliest mechanical sorters emulated the pitch fork, and this type consists of three or five troughs mounted on cranks in such a way that the straw is picked up and thrown forward by each trough in turn. This is a very simple and reliable mechanism, but it is also very bulky.

With a well-designed threshing drum, roughly 80 per cent of the grain should be sorted in the drum by passing through holes in the concave. Recent developments with axial-flow threshers have increased this to 100 per cent so that a thresher can do without the very bulky straw walkers. One feature of the axial-flow drum is that sorting is more effective at high loadings, whereas the efficiency of straw walkers falls off very rapidly as the throughput rises. For hand-fed machines, where feeding tends to be erratic, the straw walker is probably the most efficient.

Winnowing

Traditional threshing methods leave a lot of trash among the grain and separating this can require almost as much labour as the original threshing. If there is plenty of wind, the threshed material is tossed in the air using forks, shovels, baskets, etc. and the lighter chaff and straw is blown to one side while the grain falls vertically. Final cleaning may be done with a winnowing basket, which is shaken until any chaff and dirt separate at the upper edge. This is very simple and effective but, at only about 40-45kg per hour, it is slow. An alternative is to use winnowing sieves, open-weave baskets that may be suspended on tripods. They are shaken so that the grain falls through; the chaff and straw remain in the sieve.

Various types of winnowing machines are designed to create artificial wind. The simplest are hand- and pedal-operated fans: two, three or four light metal blades are rotated by hand cranks or foot pedals. Slightly more sophisticated is the fanning mill, where the fan is mounted in a wooden housing which contains sieves and screens — the grain is thus graded as well as cleaned. The fan may be manually or engine powered. Fanning mills produce a very clean sample but cannot cope with large amounts of straw, so they are more appropriate for finer winnowing.

Health and safety

Much harvesting and threshing equipment is potentially dangerous if not manufactured to an adequate standard or not used properly. The costs of equipment are sometimes kept low by omitting safety features. Threshers have been produced, for example, without the protective guard needed to take wheat into the machine and keep hands and arms out. This saves sheet metal but raises accident rates — 95 per cent of which occur while crops are being fed into the machines.

Post-harvest crop processing

Most crops need to be dried, packaged or processed into some slightly different form from that in the field. The type of crops to be considered in this section will be largely seed crops for human food, animal feed and oil extraction, with less emphasis on fruit, vegetables and fibre crops; attention will be focused on the small- to medium-scale items of equipment suitable for household or village use.

This section looks at the processes needed to increase the nutritional or market value of harvested and threshed crops. Inevitably there is the need to ensure the material is dry enough, if it is to be stored for any length of time, so the section starts with a brief look at drying and storage methods. This is a complex subject in its own right and the lack of space devoted to it in no way reflects its relative importance. Users concerned with this aspect of post-harvest processing should consult local expert advisers before investing in equipment.

This section also includes equipment designed to clean (especially) grain before and sometimes after, a milling or shelling process. These items of equipment precede grain milling and other processing equipment, which is considered in order of horsepower requirement within each category of equipment, starting with manual machinery. With this type, low efficiency is clearly undesirable even though a technique is effective; this is particularly true for oil-processing equipment.

In the majority of cases crop processing equipment will be powered by motors and these are always a vital factor in the selection of equipment, and may cost far more than the actual process machine. This is particularly so where electricity is not available and small petrol or diesel engines are required.

Grain-drying machinery

Although grain can be dried on a continuous or batch basis, it is much more convenient at low and medium scale to use the batch system. In the commoner designs the seed or grain is contained in a large rectangular box or tray. The grain should be spread evenly over the perforated plate in the bottom of the box and heated air will be blown up through a lower plenum chamber.

Typical drying rates would be 1 per cent per hour of moisture removed. The power requirement for this type of operation would be 1.5kW for 1t capacity. The fan may be diesel or electrically operated and the heat may be provided by kerosene, electricity, rice hulls, gas or other fuel. Grain can be loaded in sacks but it is usually loaded in bulk, and discharge spouts are provided with sack mounting hooks.

Air-screen seed cleaners

These machines will clean seed efficiently, removing leaf, chaff, soil and other rubbish. Small-scale versions are hand operated and are suitable for sorghum, millet, maize, soya beans and any free-flowing seed crop. Different screen sizes can be provided to suit any size of crop and usually a minimum of two screens is needed for each operation. The upper screen filters out oversize material and the lower screen filters out the undersize. The middle-sized material is blown through a winnowing section to remove the light bits of leaf, chaff, glumes and hollow seed. This machine can be used immediately after a thresher and prior to hulling, milling or resowing.

Simple winnowers are also available with an electric motor-operated fan. These will separate the light material from the heavy, simply by blowing the mass of material up into an air column. In one type, the heavy material continues upwards while the light particles are blown sideways. Another type allows the heavy material to sink to the bottom of the column. This machine is suitable both for pre-cleaning a seed crop or for separating hulled rice, coffee etc. from the husks.

Grain milling

The milling of grain and grain legumes for human and animal feed is one of the most basic of crop-processing requirements. The following paragraphs discuss the main technical characteristics of the commonest types of mill.

Plate Mill The plate mill is usually limited to about 7kW and is derived from the stone mill or quern. In the modern plate mill, two chilled iron plates are mounted on a horizontal axis so that one of the plates rotates and the grain is ground between them. The pressure between them governs the fineness of the product and is adjusted by a hand screw. The grain is usually coarsely cracked in the feed screw to the centre of the plates. Grooves in the plates decrease in depth outwards towards the periphery so that the grain is ground progressively finer until it emerges at the outer edge and falls by gravity into a sack or bowl.

This machine is also very effective in grinding wet products such as wetted maize, tomatoes, peppers and spices. Water may be added by simply pouring it into the feed section as required. Manual versions of the plate mill are available but the work is hard and throughput is only 1-2kg/h on cereals. It is more effective than pounding or rubbing stones, however, and will produce a fine meal.

Roller Mill For feeding ruminants, grain needs only to be crushed rather than ground. A roller mill which simply flattens the grain is perfectly adequate for this purpose, a 3kW machine being able to crush up to 0.5t/h of barley.

Hammer Mills These range in size from 2 to 20kW in village operation and consist essentially of a circular chamber in which beaters whirl at high speed. Around the tips of the beaters a circular perforated plate allows the shattered grain to filter through either to fall out of the base by gravity or to be sucked through a fan to an elevated delivery point. The size of the holes in the perforated plate determines the particle size and a 1mm hole size is suitable for most human foods, whereas a 3mm hole is preferred for animal feed.

Most grain crops can be ground in a hammer mill. The input to the mill can be controlled by hand in a feed tray to the centre or side of the mill. Alternatively, bulk hoppers can be mounted over the mill to give a continuous operation. The mill may be driven by a direct-mounted electric motor, by V-belt or flat belt. The simplest type is the direct-mounted, gravity-discharge mill because there are no additional belts or bearings except those of the electric motor. In this case the motor is flange-mounted on the back of the mill and the hammers are keyed directly on to the stub shaft of the motor. The flat-belt type is next to be preferred, and finally the V-belt drive type, which suffers from the problem of replacing the V-belts. The direct-drive mill needs no guards and is clearly safer.

It is also up to 20 per cent more efficient.

The hammer mill is used just as frequently for animal and poultry meal production as for human food. Oystershell, an ingredient of poultry meal, can also be ground in the hammer mill, but wear rates are much higher.

The vertical meal mixer is excellent for blending meal with concentrates or other ingredients. A vertical conical-bottomed hopper has a central screw auger which re-circulates the meal. A 2t hopper would probably have a 3kW mixer drive motor. Several companies supply a complete mill, mix and storage unit containing a feed hopper, and a hammer mill with pneumatic delivery to a vertical mixer set in a round or square hopper. This is usually a good way to buy a matched system for a reasonable price.

Health and safety

Much crop-processing equipment contains cutters, knives, rasps and so on. These are potentially dangerous if they are not properly guarded.

Motors and engines are items of inherently high speed. The machines they drive are often directly coupled to rotate at the same speed and the safety regulations developed in some countries are often totally disregarded in others.

The two major hazards are: first, unguarded belts and machinery and, secondly, poorly maintained electrical wire and connections. Careful instruction is needed in the initial stages of operation. Petrol and diesel engines need adequate exhaust pipes leading outside the building to prevent the build up of fumes.

The most important features of safety when dealing with high-speed rotational machinery (as most of the foregoing equipment is) are careful retention of guards on all belts, pulleys and transmission systems and secondly, the protection of all feed sections against probing fingers. A wise precaution is often to provide a wooden pusher to feed all mills, mixers, hullers, pulpers, etc. or at least provide a coarse guard screen for the free flowing crops. Customers or casual visitors should be kept to safe areas. This particularly includes children.

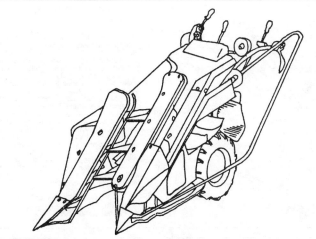

REAPER-BINDERS

Motorized reaper-binders are a development of the more usual power tiller with cutter bar. Although the reaper-binder's cutting width is smaller than that of a cutter bar mower, this is compensated for by the binding mechanism which gathers up the cut grass or cereal, and ties it into sheaves. The latter is a very time-consuming and labour-intensive operation if done by hand alone.

SUZUE BINDERS There are 2 models in this range, the 1-row, 2-wheel Bx300S, and the 2-row, 2-wheel B600DB. The binding is of the knotter and bill type and is carried out with twine.

SUZUE AGRICULTURAL MACHINERY CO. LTD.
144-2 Gomen-cho
Nankoku-shi, Kochi-ken 783
JAPAN

KOREAN BINDERS Listed here are 3 models of binder available for export

from Korea. They are the RX-550, KB-602 and HE-50A.

MODEL RX-550: air-cooled petrol engine developing 4.0hp at 4000rpm. It has a weight of 161kg, an average speed of 0.86m/sec, and a cutting width of 50cm. Manufactured by Tong Yang Moolsan Co. Ltd.

MODEL KB-602: air-cooled, 4-stroke petrol engine developing 4.5hp. It has a cutting width of 55cm and a capacity of 4ha/h. Manufactured by Kukje Machinery Co. Ltd.

MODEL HE-50A: a 168kg implement driven by a 4-stroke petrol engine which develops 4.2hp at 3400rpm. An average working speed of 0.85m/sec and working width of 45cm may be expected. Manufactured by Dae Dong Ind. Co. Ltd.
These three binders are all available through:

KOREA TRADE PROMOTION CORPORATION
C.P.O. Box 1621, Seoul
KOREA

'MOTORSCYTHE' SWATHER

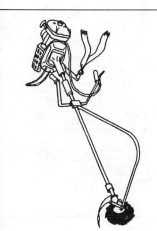

The Motorscythe Swather is a lightweight, heavy-duty rotary cutter suitable for tasks ranging from land clearance to harvesting small cereal plots.
The swather weighs 10kg and is equipped with the following:
● 35cc petrol engine
● shoulder harness
● double-handed control bar
● swathing bat for clearance of standing crops into rows
● tooth whirl blade with guard.
The interested reader is referred to the description of land clearance equipment in Section 13 (Miscellaneous) where a range of brush cutters similar to the 'Motorscythe' is listed.

ALVAN BLANCH DEV. CO. LTD.
Chelworth
Malmesbury, Wilts. SN16 9SG
U.K.

5HP GRASS CUTTERS

Motorized grass cutters in the 5hp range have the advantage of being versatile enough for use in quite difficult terrain, while having sufficient power and capacity for working in quite large areas. The 3 models described here are manufactured in West Germany and Austria and are available for export.

THE AGRIA 5300 This model (illustrated) is able to harvest grass at a rate of up to 0.3ha/h, the Agria 5300 has the following characteristics: combined speed control and engine cut-out mechanism; forward, reverse and idling gears controlled by a single coupling lever; 4-stroke, 5hp petrol engine with recoil starter; pneumatic tyres or cage wheels; independent traction and mowing mechanisms; fingerless 100cm wide cutter bar; total weight 75kg.

AGRIA-WERKE GmbH
Postfach 1147
7108 Möckmühl
W. GERMANY

THE REFORM 115 DIESEL MOTOR MOWER A very sophisticated machine able to carry out a range of tasks in addition to grass cutting. The mower is driven by a Lombardini diesel LDA 520, 4-stroke, 325cc, air-cooled engine which develops 5DIN HP at 3000rpm. It has a fuel consumption of less than 1 litre/h and is equipped with 2 forward and 2 reverse gears. The grass cutting capacity of the 115 motor mower is enhanced by a range of 3 different cutter bars, each suited to certain conditions and grass types. These give cutting widths of 1.4-1.7m. Also available are additional wheel attachments for extra stability (e.g. cage wheels).

REFORM-WERKE BAUER & CO. GmbH
Postfach 192
Haidestraße 40
A-4600 Wels
AUSTRIA

BM 100/2G This mower is the largest of a range of three produced by Gutbrod. It has a cutting width of 100cm and a Gutbrod 2-stroke motor with an output of about 3.7kW.

GUTBROD-WERKE GmbH
Postfach Box 60
6601 Saarbrücken-Bübingen
W. GERMANY

THRESHERS

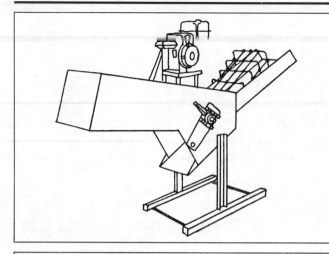

ATS MIDGET THRESHER MKII A

Suitable for threshing wheat, barley, oats, beans, peas, sorghum, maize and rice, the Midget consists of a 6 beater, rasp bar drum with sealed bearings. The construction is of heavy plate with a lightweight feed chute and discharge hood over a simple fixed grid straw separator and grain chute. The power required is 3hp and capacity is up to 500kg/h for dry wheat. The overall weight is 127kg. Various concave attachments are available for maize, groundnuts and sorghum, including an extra pulley to reduce the drum speed. A screen separator is also available. Alvan Blanch produce a wide range of threshers, including the larger Master Midget which can be used as a peg drum thresher as well as a rasp bar, making it ideal for threshing high quality rice.

ALVAN BLANCH DEV. CO. LTD.
Chelworth
Malmesbury, Wilts. SN16 9SG
U.K.

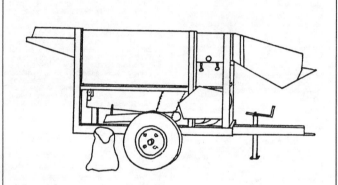

MOBILE THRESHERS

AMAR MULTICROP THRESHER This is a raspbar thresher suitable for all cereals, soybeans etc. It requires 10hp, and has a capacity of 6-10 quintals/h for wheat, and 25-35 quintals/h for maize. The overall weight is 640kg.

AMAR AGRICULTURAL IMPLEMENTS WORKS
Amar Street, Gill Road
Janta Nagar, Ludhiana-141003
INDIA

VICON THRESHER ST-45 The ST-45 is fitted with a rasp bar drum, and can be equipped with wheels for trailing, or a yoke for bullock draught. It has a power requirement of 10hp, and a capacity ranging from 1000kg/h for wheat, to 2000kg/h for maize. The overall weight is 790kg.

VICON LTD.
K.R. Puram — Whitefield Road
Mahadevapura Post
Bangalore 560 048, Karnataka
INDIA

MINORETTE AND MINOR THRESHERS The minorette (illustrated) has a power requirement of 7.5hp. It can be fitted with either a peg drum, consisting of 12 bars each with 5 pegs, or a rasp bar drum, consisting of 6 beaters. The overall weight is 900kg. Capacity, based on average dry wheat, can reach 1000kg/h. The Minor is a larger thresher weighing 1400kg. Like the minorette it can be fitted with a rasp bar or a peg drum. Capacity can reach 2000kg/h. The minor thresher features a grain elevator consisting of a bucket and roller chain with single bagging-off chute. It is constructed from steel and mounted on a robust steel chassis.

ALVAN BLANCH DEV. CO. LTD.
Chelworth
Malmesbury, Wilts. SN16 9SG
U.K.

SMALL MOTORIZED GRASS CUTTERS

Alpina manufacture 2 small motorized grass cutters.

THE MODEL HOBBY 202 This consists of a tubular transmission shaft to which is attached the engine, handle-bars, ground wheels and cutter bar mower. It is a lightweight implement (18kg) suited to steep and inaccessible areas of up to 0.2ha. The engine is 2-stroke with an 85cc displacement. This motivates the cutter bar which has an adjustable working height and width of 80cm.

THE MODEL ELITE 402 Although this model (illustrated) is equipped with a similar 85cc, 2-stroke engine and 80cm cutter bar, its heavier construction (25kg) and additional land wheel allow it to be used on large areas. An output of up to 0.1ha/h may be achieved.

ALPINA
31015 Conegliano, Treviso
ITALY

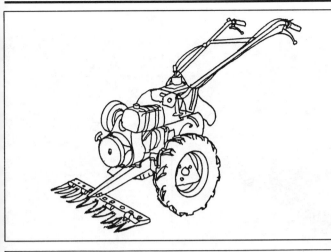

GRASS CUTTERS

The grass cutters described here are similar in form to those of 5HP listed on this page. Their primary function is grass harvesting although they may also be adapted for other mechanized functions. Here, the interested reader requiring information on multi-purpose power tillers, many of which include grass cutter bar attachments, is referred to the relevant pages on motorized tillage in Section 1 of this Guide.

THE MONROTILLER MOTOR SCYTHE This model (illustrated), although designed principally for grass cutting work, may be adapted to perform a range of functions in soil tillage and traction. Accessories include:

- extra diameter pneumatic wheels
- primary tillage equipment
- tool frame attachment
- trailer hitch (sprung or heavy-duty)
- blanking plate for side PTO

MECHGARD LTD.
Great Gransden, Sandy
Bedfordshire SG19 3AY, U.K.

THE BEBY MOTOR SCYTHE An implement with the following technical characteristics:

- 5HP (DIN), 4-stroke petrol engine
- PTO (frontal)
- mowing bar adjustable up to 70cm
- weight 78kg
- spraying pump attachment.

BARBIERI, SpA
Via Circonvallazione, 19
36040 Sossano, Vicenza
ITALY

THE FORMICA 2 M This is similar to the Beby motor scythe, this model has technical specifications which include:

- 5hp, 2-stroke engine
- 2 forward speeds
- adjustable handlebars
- weight 55kg
- lister, trailer and cultivator.

M.A.B. DI GUIDO BOCCHINI
Via Erbosa, 47030 Gatteo (F.O.), ITALY

STANDARD THRESHERS

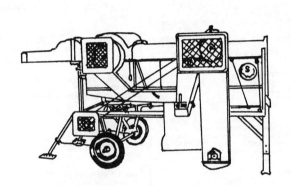

STANDARD UNIVERSAL THRESHER RD IVa This machine (illustrated above) is suitable for threshing all cereals. It consists of a peg-threshing drum and adjustable concaves. It has a power requirement of 5-8hp, and an overall weight of 470kg.

STANDARD RICE THRESHER IIa Adaptable for hand, foot or motor drive, this thresher is equipped with a toothed drum and toothed concave. It does not have a cleaner and straw shaker attachments. Power requirement is 3-5 hp, and overall weight is 330kg. (Illustrated below).

STANDARD GmbH
Postfach 1160
3118 Bad Bevensen
W. GERMANY

PLOT THRESHER

This small thresher was specially developed for threshing different grains in experimental plots. It incorporates a special air device which enables the operator to adjust the air flow ensuring efficient separation of the chaff from the seed. The engine requires 7hp, and the overall weight is 480kg. The thresher is equipped with two tyred wheels and tow bar.

SWANSON MACHINE CO.
20-26 E. Columbia Avenue
Champaign, Illinois 61820
U.S.A.

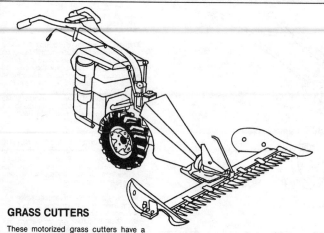

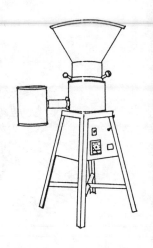

GRASS CUTTERS

These motorized grass cutters have a power output greater than 5hp. They are equipped with a front cutter bar.

CORTINA/C GRASS CUTTER This model is shown in the illustration with a symetrically attached cutter bar. A lateral version is also available. It has a 10hp petrol or diesel engine with power take-off and 3 speeds, including reverse. Other attachments include a ridger, spray and irrigation pump, plough, trailer and circular saw.

BARBIERI, SpA
Via Circonvallazione, 19
36040 Sossano, Vicenza
ITALY

GRASS CUTTER MODEL 131 Available with either central or lateral cutter bars. The power output is 5, 7, or 9hp, and the gear box provides 3 speeds, 2 forward and 1 reverse. The cutting width is from 650 to 1270mm.

BERTOLINI MACCHINE AGRICOLE,
SpA
42100 Reggio Emilia
Via Guicciardi 7
ITALY

790 MOTOR SCYTHE Available with either central or lateral cutter bars. The petrol engine has displacement from 300 to 350cc. At 3600rpm there are 3 forward speeds from 2.3 to 10.2kph and one reverse. Other attachments include: circular saw, compressor, various mowing bars, harvesting attachment, grinder.

O.M. FERRARI, SpA
Via Valbrina 19
42045 Luzzara (R.E.)
ITALY

GRASS CUTTERS MODELS GB 444 and GB 495 The GB 444 has a 4-stroke, 127cc petrol engine. It has a central cutter bar and cutting width of 70cm. The GB 495 is a larger model with a 4-stroke, 161cc engine and cutting width of 110m.

GRANJA, S.A.
109 route de Toulouse
31270 Cugnaux
FRANCE

VERTICAL AXIS GRINDING MILLS

A range of heavy duty vertical axis grinding mills suitable for small commercial use. The S.A.M.A.P. model is illustrated above.

KISAN KRISHI YANTRA UDYOG
64 Moti Bhawan
Collectorganj, Kanpur 208 001
INDIA

S.A.M.A.P.
1 rue du Molin BP 1
Andolsheim
Neuf-Brisach, 68600
FRANCE

A.B.C. HANSEN COMP A/S
Hauchsvej 14, Post Box 3054
DK 1508 Copenhagen V
DENMARK

SHERPUR POTATO GRADER

The potatoes are fed in at one end, carried along by rubber spools, and sorted into as many grades as desired. Power requirement is 2hp and capacity can reach 2800kg/h with 3 or 4 persons operating the machine.

UNION FORGINGS
Focal Point
Sherpur, Ludhiana, Punjab
INDIA

SMALL FLOUR MILLS

TYPE 'BABY' HAMMER MILLS These multipurpose mills (illustrated left) have a very high rotation speed in the mill chamber of 6000rpm. The 6 reversible hammers are 8mm wide. It is built entirely of steel. Powered by motors from 4-7.5hp, or by a tractor PTO, most models are stand-alone but one model comes complete with a 450 litre bin on which the mill is mounted.

ELECTRA
47170 Poudenas
FRANCE

GFC — 308 DISC MILL This mill rotates at 4600rpm, powered by a 4hp electric motor. It is similar in appearance to the Electra Baby Mill but with the motor mounted at the base of the legs.

CHINA NATIONAL AGRICULTURAL MACHINERY
Import and Export Corporation
26 South Yeutan Street, Beijing
CHINA

HAND-OPERATED FRUIT PRESSES AND CRUSHERS

Below are listed three manufacturers of different types of presses and fruit crushers.

'SIEGERIN' FRUIT AND BERRY PRESSES This lever-operated press when operated by one person achieves an hourly output of 25 litres of juice.

THE 'SIEGERIN' CRUSHERS These both grind and crush in one operation. Output for apples is 150kg/h. The illustration (left) shows the crusher mounted on top of the fruit press.

RAUCH LANDMASCHINENFABRIK GmbH
Postfach 1107, Sinzheim 7573
W. GERMANY

FRUIT AND BERRY PRESS & CRUSHER Two models available. One is a vertical, batch, screw press which compresses fruit within a barrel. The second is a horizontal axis crusher. The models are similar to those of Rauch.

COMPANHIA INDUSTRIAL DE FUNDIÇÃO
17 Rua de São João 27, 4000 Porto
PORTUGAL

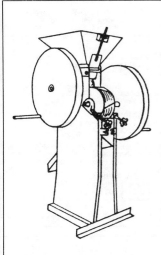

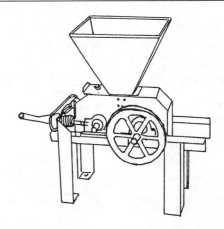

HAND-OPERATED ROLLER MILL

This roller mill has been designed as part of a seed oil extraction system. In principle its action is similar to the motorized roller mills which follow. It is powered by two people operating the hand cranks at either side of the mill. A third person is required to feed the mill and to relieve those operating it. Reasonable throughputs can be achieved.

TRAAS METAAL B.V.
Groene Kruisstraat 3
4414 A L Waarde (2)
NETHERLANDS

SMALL ROLLER MILLS

'LITTLE BRITCHES' ROLLER MILL Suitable for the small feeder, with a power requirement of 1hp and a capacity of 350-700kg/h for oats and 450-750kg/h for maize (illustrated).

H.C. DAVIS SONS MFG. CO. INC.
P.O. Box 395
Bonner Springs, Kansas 66012
U.S.A.

DRY GRAIN CRUSHING MILL Capacity ranges from 100-250kg/h with a power requirement of 2hp.

STE COMIA-FAO SA
27 bd de Châteaubriant, BP 91
35500 Vetré
FRANCE

YN221 DOUBLE-ROLLER GRINDER & 6F-1728A MILL MODELS With power requirements of 5 and 3kW, output is 400kg/h (based on cotton seed) and 120-140kg/h of grain respectively.

CHINA NATIONAL AGRICULTURAL MACHINERY
Import and Export Corporation
26 South Yeutan Street, Beijing
CHINA

MODEL FG-61 A feed grinder with a power requirement of 2-4hp and a capacity of 200-325kg/h.

CECOCO
P.O. Box 8
Ibaraki City, Osaka 567
JAPAN

TYPE A 180 An economical 3hp electric motor yields 300-700 litres/h.

ELECTRA
47170 Poudenas
FRANCE

GRAIN ROLLER TYPE GH 374 A 3hp mill with capacity of 200-400kg grain/h.

ETS. A. GAUBERT
22 rue Gambetta, BP 24
16700 Ruffec
FRANCE

MILLS

POWER-OPERATED GRINDING MILLS (FREE STANDING)

A range of sturdy free-standing mills suitable for grinding most grains. Outputs range from approximately 100-600kg/h, with the capacity of the machines largely determined by the moisture content of the material. These mills are commonly driven by electric motors from 1-8hp.

'JUNIOR' & 'SENIOR' 170 FLOUR MILLS 1-2hp and 3hp with capacities of 100-200kg and 150-400kg respectively.

ETS. A. GAUBERT
22 rue Gambetta
BP 24, 16700 Ruffec
FRANCE

ARGOUD VERTICAL MILLS Four mills from 2-5hp with capacities ranging between 80-450kg/h.

S.E.C.A.
38260 La Cote St. André
FRANCE

FLOUR MILL B31 A 4-6hp motor gives a capacity of 400kg/h (illustrated above right).

STE. COMIA-FAO SA
27 bd. de Châteaubriant, BP 91
35500 Vitré
FRANCE

SUPERB MILL A power requirement of 5hp gives an output of 500-600kg/h.

BENTALL SIMPLEX LTD
P.O. Box 10
Normanby Park
Industrial Estate
Scunthorpe
South Humberside, U.K.

AMUDA FLAT PLATE GRINDING MILL 1A A capacity of 180kg/h for dry material at 4-5hp.

RAJAN UNIVERSAL EXPORTS (MFRS.) PVT. LTD.
Post Bag 250, Madras 600 001
INDIA

AB CHELWORTH MILL Capacity approximately 250kg/h when driven by 5.5hp electric motor.

ALVAN BLANCH DEV. CO. LTD.
Chelworth
Malmesbury, Wilts. SN16 9SG
U.K.

A320 & SILEX NO. 3 CEREAL MILLS Capacities approximately 600-1000kg/h and 350-600kg/h when driven by 4hp and 6-8hp motor, respectively.

RENSON ET CIE
BP 23, 59550 Landrecies
FRANCE

PREMIER 1A and 2A GRINDING MILLS Output up to 300kg/h with a power requirement of 5-7hp.

R. HUNT & CO. LTD.
52, High Street
Earls Coon
Colchester
Essex
U.K.

D.S. STYLE GRINDING MILL A 6-8hp mill with a capacity of 230-270kg/h.

DANDEKAR BROTHERS
(Engineers & Founders)
Sangli-Shivaji Nagar, 416 416
Maharashtra
INDIA

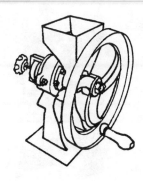

SMALL GRAIN MILLS

TYPE B100 This mill (left) is made of cast iron with steel plates. A screw adjusts for fineness of flour. Recommended speed is 80-150rpm. Output can be up to 30kg/h.

S.E.C.A.
38260 La Cote St. André
FRANCE

CORN CRUSHER A similar model is produced by Renson. The hand-wheel is 380mm diameter by 40mm wide.

RENSON ET CIE
BP 23, 59550 Landrecies
FRANCE

MINI-GRINDER This grinder (right) has interchangeable grinding wheels, 90mm in diameter made of special cast iron.

ETS. A. GAUBERT
22 rue Gambetta
BP 24, 16700 Ruffec
FRANCE

ATLAS NO. 3 HANDPOWER GRINDING MILL

Hand powered 2-operator grinding mill (left) for all kinds of dry grain. 190mm diameter grinding plates. Output up to 20kg/h. Mounted on cast iron column or four steel legs.

R. HUNT & CO. LTD.
52, High Street
Earls Coon
Colchester
Essex
U.K.

AB MINI MILL

The AB Mini Mill (right) is the smallest of the plate mills, designed for easy hand operation with a 380mm diameter flywheel and specially hardened cast steel. The flywheel and handle can be removed and be replaced by a 0.5hp electric motor. Output is between 22 and 30kg/h for the hand operated version and 30 to 100kg/h for the motorized version.

The weights of these bench mounted models are 12 and 17kg respectively.

ALVAN BLANCH DEV. CO. LTD.
Chelworth
Malmesbury, Wilts, SN16 9SG, U.K.

FLOOR-MOUNTED HAMMER MILLS

5X HAMMER MILL President mills come with a wide range of standard fittings including 4 different mesh screens. The 5X (illustrated above) engine capacity is 4-5.5kW; conveyor length is 35m and throughput about 250kg/h. The 10X engine capacity is 5.5-7.5(-11)kW; conveyor length is 45m and throughput about 450kg/h. A fully automated intake control can be mounted to ensure the motor does not overload.

PRESIDENT MØLLERIMASKINER A/S
DK-4300 Holbaek
DENMARK

BABY MIRACLE MILL 4 versions of this model are available. Mill chamber speed 6000rpm; output 250 to 400kg/h.

S.E.C.A.
38260 La Cote St. André
FRANCE

SERIES F6 The mill chamber is 15cm in diameter. The power required ranges from 7.5 to 15hp using 8 or 12 hammers.

ELECTRA
47170 Poudenas
FRANCE

STOCK MILL The stockmill grinds maize, cassava, all cereals, oyster shells, peas,

beans, rice, corn cobs, straw, chalk etc. It has a large diameter rotor and a mill chamber lined with percussion bars. A blower system enhances the flow of meal through the screen and constantly cools the mill chamber. It has a 75 litre hopper and the feed is protected by a powerful permanent magnet, which traps metal objects. Shock absorbers are supplied as standard equipment. The specially tempered steel hammers may be turned round so as to use all four corners. This makes it possible to mill over 120 tonnes of cereal before they need replacing. Output varies according to the power available, either a 7.5 or 10hp electric motor or a 12hp diesel motor can be provided. For five screen sizes, 0.8mm, output of maize is 150-220kg/h or 525kg/h for cassava. For coarse screen sizes, 5mm output can rise to 950kg/h for maize. Shipping volume is 2.2m³.

ASE EUROPE N.V.
Century Centre
de Keyserlei 58, Box 1
B-2018 Antwerp
BELGIUM

ESSEX MAJOR HAMMER MILLS Hammer mill available in four sizes 3, 5.5, 7.5 and 10hp. The largest (illustrated in the introduction to this section) is capable of grinding over one tonne per hour. Push button start and automatic stop provided. Swing hammer design takes only 30 seconds to switch production from fine to coarse meal — the time taken to change the screens (2.5, 3.0 and 5.00mm). High volume fan will deliver ground meal 20m

Model hp	Output of ground barley through 3mm screen kg/h
3	100
5.5	200
7.5	275
10	375

CHRISTY & NORRIS LTD.
Kings Road, Chelmsford
Essex, CMI 1SA
U.K.

ALVAN BLANCH DEV. CO. LTD.
Chelworth
Malmesbury, Wilts. SN16 9SG
U.K.

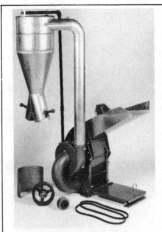

HAMMER MILLS WITH CYCLONE BAGGERS

The manufacturers listed below all produce a range of hammer mills similar to that illustrated (above) made by C.S. Bell Co. The power ranges are given, where known. All include blowers which deliver the meal or flour into a cyclone bagger, on left, which usually has two bagging discharge spouts. Capacities of the cyclone can be adjusted to suit the client. The photo (above right) is a view inside the hammer mill showing the staggered, free-swinging hammer arrangement with the blower on its left.

BLOWER DISCHARGE HAMMER MILL 3 models: 3, 5, 15hp.

C.S. BELL CO.
170 W. Davis Street
Box 291, Tiffin, OH 44883
U.S.A.

STANDARD HAMMER MILLS Power required: 7.5 to 50hp.

KONGSKILDE U.K. LTD.
Holt, Norfolk NR25 6EE
U.K.

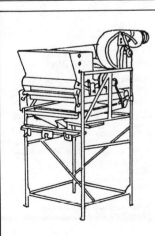

MEDIUM CAPACITY 2-SIEVE PRE-CLEANER

The model 2SA/4 is a 2-sieve single aspiration pre-cleaner with an output of up to 4 tonnes/h. It is more efficient for cleaning dried grain than wet grain. It is constructed entirely of steel with an aspiration fan V-belt driven by a 1hp electric motor (alternative engine drive available) also driving oscillating mechanism of the sieve shoes. Grain is fed into the input hopper and falls onto the top screen where the aspiration fan is regulated to remove the lighter particles which are expelled. The top sieve removes straws and sticks which are directed down a rubbish chute. The bottom sieve removes smaller particles of rubbish from the grain.

ALVAN BLANCH DEV. CO. LTD.
Chelworth
Malmesbury, Wilts. SN16 9SG
U.K.

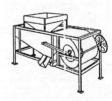

3 SIEVE SEPARATOR

The 3SW/2 (illustrated) is a hand-operated 3-sieve winnower which may be driven by an electric motor or engine. A wide choice of screens are available for different seeds. The capacity is 2 tonne grain/h.

ALVAN BLANCH DEV. CO. LTD.
Chelworth
Malmesbury, Wilts. SN16 9SG
U.K.

POWER-OPERATED GRINDING MILLS (BENCH MODELS)

These mills work on a similar principle to the hand-operated grinding mills, but are driven by a small motor. Below are listed the manufacturers of various types of grinding mill.

AMUDA DOMESTIC MILL Driven by a 0.5-1hp electric motor or a 1.95hp Villiers Engine, this cast-iron mill has an output of 8-20kg/h. It can also be adjusted for hand operation.

RAJAN UNIVERSAL EXPORTS (MFRS.) PVT. LTD.
Post Bag 250, Madras 600 001
INDIA

CHILLED BURR TYPE FLOUR GRINDING MILLS General-purpose mills suitable for grinding all grains and also chemical materials. Capacity ranges from 60-160kg/h for Type D (0.25-0.5hp) up to 200-900kg/h for Type A (3hp).

NUMBER 60 MODEL POWER MILL Steel alloy mill suitable for grinding all dry grains. It is powered by a 1-2hp electric motor and has an output of 45-130kg/h.

C.S. BELL CO.
170 W. Davis Street
Box 291, Tiffin OH 44883
U.S.A.

PREMIER 127 GRINDING MILL Small mill for wet or dry grinding of grain, tomatoes, peppers, spices, etc. Hand-operated auger feed to enable multiple grinding for extra fineness. Operated by petrol/kerosene engines or electric motor, capacity up to 100kg/h (illustrated above).

R. HUNT & CO. LTD.
52, High Street
Earls Coon
Colchester, Essex
U.K.

'WOLF' GENERAL PURPOSE PULPER

Tigges manufacture a small range of general purpose pulpers for fruit processing.

TIGGES GEBR. GmbH & CO. KG
2 Sünninghausen
4740 Oelde
W. GERMANY

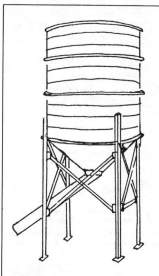

HORIZONTAL BLADE ROOT CUTTERS

POWER TURNIP CUTTER The horizontal rim drive turnip cutter is produced by both Alvan Blanch and Elbar. It is a new design with 760mm diameter bowl to cope with large roots. The machine is practically free from maintenance costs; fitted with ball bearings throughout which ensures an easy silent drive.
It can be driven by a 1.5hp electric motor, or a 1.5hp engine. Finger piece knives can be fitted in addition to the slicing knives. Roots are cut to a uniform 19mm slice.

ALVAN BLANCH DEV. CO. LTD.
Chelworth
Malmesbury, Wilts. SN16 9SG
U.K.

BLAIR ENG. LTD.
Rattray, Blairgowrie PH10 7DN
U.K.

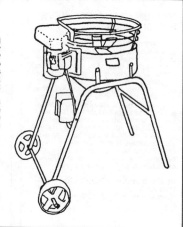

ELEVATED GRAIN AND MEAL STORAGE BINS

Elevated storage bins may be used for keeping either grain or animal feeds dry and safe from vermin. The outlet is situated at the conical base and has the advantage of being self-cleaning. The fact that the outlet is situated above ground level is convenient for loading and distribution operations. The Cossul bins are illustrated above. A wide range of storage capacities are available.

COSSUL & CO. PVT. LTD.
123/367 Industrial Area
Fazalgunj, Kanpur, U.P.
INDIA

LAW EXPORT LTD.
Quarry Road, Chipping Sodbury
Bristol BS17 6AX
U.K.

BLOC SERIES ELECTRICAL GRINDERS

As part of a wide range of mills and milling equipment, this small mill can be supplied with a plate or hammers. It has a 5.5hp motor at 3000rpm. It is suitable for attachment to a grain bin, but legs can be supplied.

LAW EXPORT LTD.
Quarry Road, Chipping Sodbury
Bristol BS17 6AX
U.K.

BATCH DRIERS

IRRI BATCH DRIER These driers are constructed of wood or steel and can dry 1 tonne of paddy in 4 to 6 hours (illustrated above).
Technical specifications:
power; 3 hp petrol engine or 2hp electric motor
weight: fan and kerosene burner 40kg; drying bin 220kg (steel), 200kg (wood)
length, width, height (cm): fan and burner 90, 110, 60; steel bin 277, 190, 92; wooden bin 254, 254, 109
grain depth; 33-46cm
fan; 47cm diameter, vane axial type
airflow; 0.85cu m/sec.
air temperature; 43°C
fuel consumption; 0.75 litres petrol/h, 2.0 litres kerosene/h
A rice hull furnace may be used as an alternative to the kerosene burner

KAUNLARAN INDUSTRIES
Calamba, Laguna
PHILIPPINES

JCCE INDUSTRIES
242 Mayondon
Los Baños, Laguna
PHILIPPINES

GRAIN DRYER Model KB-6D requires a 2 hp electric motor or a 3-4hp engine. The capacity is 1300kg and drying rate is up to 1.2 per cent/h. A larger model with slower drying rate is also available.

YAMAMOTO MFG. CO. LTD.
813-17 Tendo-ko
Tendo-shi, Yamagata ken 994
JAPAN

CROP DRIER A large fan for drying seeds, nuts, vegetables, fish, wood, hay etc. Four models are available.

R.A. LISTER FARM EQUIPMENT LTD.
Long Street, Dursley
Gloucestershire GL11 4HF
U.K.

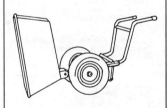

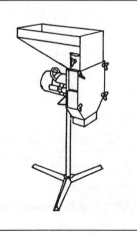

SMALL HAMMER MILLS

These motor-driven stand-alone hammer mills can be used for grinding grain especially for animal and poultry feed. They require a power input of between 1.5 to 3hp provided either by an electric or petrol-driven motor. The rapidly rotating and swinging hammers reduce the particle size of the dry material until fine enough to pass through the interchangeable perforated screens.

MINI MILL Electra produce a range of mills with outputs of between 80 and 300kg/h according to the fineness of screen. The mini mill is illustrated left.

ELECTRA
47170 Poudenas
FRANCE

POPULAR HAMMER MILL This is a 3hp electrically-powered hammer mill.

SCOTMEC LTD.
1 Whitfield Drive
Heathfield
Ayr KAH 9RX
U.K.

THE 'MAUA' TROLLEY

The 'Maua' Trolley is a tipping barrow with a 100-litre capacity reinforced container. It is supported on an iron chassis and two solid-tyred wheels, the 'foot' being centralized for maximum stability while stationary. The tubular steel handles given an overall maximum length of 1.18 metres while maximum height and width are 0.59 and 0.75 metres respectively.

PONTAL MATERIAL RODANTE S.A.
Vila Independência, Caixa Postal 8333
01.000 — São Paulo, SP
BRAZIL

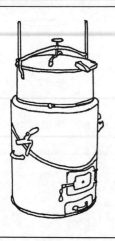

FARM STEAMERS H-020/0 & H-022/1

These two models steam potatoes for animal feed, and also boil water, use solid fuel, and can be operated inside or outside. The larger model has a boiling capacity of 100 litres and can steam 60kg of fresh potatoes, whereas the smaller model can boil 63 litres and can steam 48kg of potatoes. Other specifications:

	H-020/0	H-022/1
volume of water used (litres)	4	10
coal required for single lot (kg)	2.5	4.5
average steaming time (min)	40	45
burner grid area (sq.cm)	600	600

Manufactured by Agromet Dolzamet, Chojnow and available through:

AGROMET MOTOIMPORT
Foreign Trade Enterprise
P.O. Box 990, Warsaw
POLAND

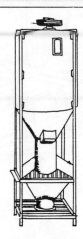

VERTICAL FEED MIXERS

Listed below are various manufacturers of different types of vertical feed mixers.

RATION MIXER 3 models are available in the range 600-2000kg/h output. They can be run by electricity (1-3hp), petrol (4.9hp) or diesel oil (4-7hp) (illustrated left).

NOGUEIRA IRMÃOS SA
Rua XV de Novembro 781
P.O. Box 7
13970 — 1 Itapira, São Paulo
BRAZIL

VERTICAL MIXERS Manufacturers of similar mixers in the range 3-9hp include:

A. KISLUK
Industrial Zone
Afula Elit 18101 P.O. Box 195
ISRAEL

LAW EXPORT LTD.
Quarry Road, Chipping Sodbury
Bristol BS17 6AX
U.K.

MOBILE CONVEYORS

The 'Ravenna' conveyor (pictured left) is an all-purpose conveyor available in standard 4-12 m lengths. The conveyor belt, which runs at about 0.9 m per second, is supplied in either 30 or 65 cm widths, and is treaded according to the users' needs. The drive unit can be either AC, DC, petrol or diesel motor, while the height may be adjusted by cable winch.

HINGHAUS MASCHINENFABRIK
GmbH
Kampenstraße 9, 4804 Versmold
Westfalia
W. GERMANY

Also available is a mobile screw conveyor. With a choice of diameters (100 mm or 135 mm), and variable length (3-10m), and an output of 4-15 tonnes per hour can be obtained according to the slope setting.

MASCHINENFABRIK HEGER GmbH
Zaberstraße 26, 7033 Herrenberg 1
W. GERMANY

WATER BARROWS

The galvanized container pivots on a horizontal axis and is manufactured with a pouring lip. Container capacities available are 100 litres and 150 litres. The chassis is of tubular steel and has two wheels with solid rubber, or, (for models produced by G. Elt), pneumatic tyres.

GEEST OVERSEAS MECHANISATION LTD.
Marsh Lane, Boston
Lincolnshire PE21 7RP
U.K.

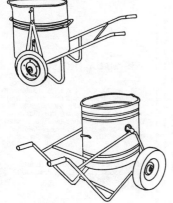

DYNAMILL

The Dynamill can be mounted on a flour or meal hopper as shown in the illustration above. This model available in 7.5 or 10hp versions with outputs from 200 (fine milling) to 2000 (crushing)kg/h. Other versions available.

ASE EUROPE N.V.
Century Centre
De Keyserlei 58, Box 1
B-2018 Antwerp
BELGIUM

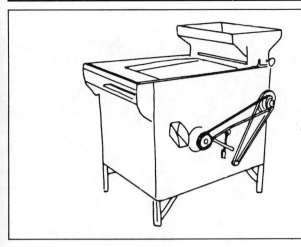

SEED GRADER

The Hindsons Seed Grader cleans and grades wheat, gram, maize and barley. Its throughput is between 600 and 1100kg/h, with a power consumption of 0.4hp. It has a voltage requirement of 220-250V.

It is made of mild steel with overall dimensions of 1375mm (length) × 1480mm (height) × 880mm (width).

4 screens are provided, two of which are in use at any one time. They have circular holes of the following diameters: 2.8mm, 3.2mm, 3.6mm and 4.4mm. They are provided with a brush cleaner.

The hopper has a capacity of 66kg of wheat. A side-plate is provided for regulating the feed to the screens.

Movement is controlled by a rack and pinion arrangement. The blower is driven by 2 V-belts.

HINDSONS PVT. LTD.
The Lower Mall
Patiala 147 001, Punjab
INDIA

Appendix 1
Water-lifting pumps and other equipment

Water is a primary requirement for securing basic food supplies through crop, livestock and forestry production systems. In addition, sufficient safe drinking water is essential for the well-being of human beings. Its provision may be a simple or complicated matter depending on the circumstances of each situation. Sometimes it may be possible to collect rainfall or run-off and distribute it by gravity to the intended point of use. More often, however, water lifting will be necessary in order to move water from the source to where it is needed. Ever since the dawn of civilization people have raised water both for domestic and agricultural needs and some types of water-lifting devices are known to have been in use for 2,000 years or more.

In its broadest sense, the term pump can be used to describe any device for raising water, whether a traditional method such as scoop or rope and bucket or the most modern high-speed rotodynamic machine. A great variety of pumping equipment has been built over the centuries to meet the requirements of specific situations. History shows that water-pumping technology changes in response to developments in power supply. Slow-speed reciprocating piston pumps driven by water-wheels or beam engines were replaced by higher speed rotary pumps powered by turbine machinery. Centrifugal pumps which have reached a high level of development are now used extensively in industrialized countries, because suitable prime movers, such as high-speed engines and electric motors, are widely available.

One of the most important points concerning the water source is whether the water level is within the practical limit or 'lift capability' of the pump. Most pumps which rely on suction for their operation cannot lift water higher than about 6 or 7m and the practical solution in this situation is to position the pump below ground so that it is closer to the water level or even submerged. Apart from the distinction between low and high lift (or shallow well and deep well) which determines where the pump should be mounted, it is also necessary to know the exact magnitude of the head in order to calculate the power required to pump the desired amount of water and to estimate the cost of doing so. It is the head during pumping which determines the power requirement. When water is pumped very slowly, the relevant head for power calculation is simply the difference in level between the outlet (typically the pump spout) and the water surface. At higher capacities, the head may increase because of friction caused by the water flowing through the pipework or because the water level is lowered. If the water level in a well falls significantly at the required pumping rate, even though the yield may be adequate, consideration should be given to the use of smaller pumps on two or more dispersed wells in order to ensure pumping through a lower head. In such cases, the power required and the associated capital and running costs of using several smaller pumps — either in parallel to deliver the required quantity of water or in series to meet the required head — should be compared with the single pump option.

Power sources and water requirements

Energy for water lifting may be obtained directly from the sun, wind or water or indirectly from plants and fossil fuels converted into human, animal, engine or electrical power. The power available from these different sources, combined with the depth from which the water must be raised, imposes practical limitations on the quantity of water that can be raised in a given time and consequently has a major bearing on the choice of pump and prime mover combination for a particular purpose. For example, a handpump lifting water from 5m can provide approximately 2.5m³/h under continuous manual operation. By contrast, a small engine or motor-driven pump of say 2.5kW could provide the same water requirements in approximately five minutes as a handpump could, operated throughout an eight-hour day. The table below shows the output from human muscle power. The daily irrigation requirement for 1ha of grain would satisfy the domestic water needs of several thousand people or a similar number of livestock. This illustrates the 'thirsty' nature of irrigation, which if it is dependent on pumps will be equally demanding on energy. Before deciding to invest in pumped irrigation it is therefore advisable to investigate carefully the viability of alternatives such as improved rain-fed systems or gravity-flow irrigation. Whichever technical solution is chosen it is essential to consider the efficient management and economic use of water; evidence shows that the poor performance of many irrigation schemes stems from fundamental weaknesses in planning and management.

Human power output (watts).		
Muscle group(s) involved	Sustained (up to 6 or 7 hrs per day) with short rests as and when required	10 to 15 mins	Few mins
Mainly arms and shoulders	30W	60W	70W
All body (arms and shoulders, back and legs — non-pedalling)	40 to 60W	70W	100W
Pedalling	75W	180W	300W

Human muscle power Compared to other alternatives the capital and running costs of muscle-powered equipment are low provided there is minimal opportunity cost for the labour. However, the low power availability limits its application to lifting small amounts of water from deep wells and boreholes for domestic use or proportionally larger amounts from shallow wells for irrigating small plots.

Water power Water power is derived from the energy contained in flowing or falling water. Its great attraction is that of usually being continuously available — although fluctuations will naturally occur with changes in river flow. Several types of water wheel and turbine are available for utilizing this power. The choice of device will depend on the available head of water, and technical and economic considerations at each particular site. Automatic hydraulic ram pumps, for example, are totally different from wheels and turbines; they are designed to exploit the phenomenon of water hammer to force a small proportion of the water flowing through the pump to a higher elevation.

Solar power Solar-powered water-pumping systems are totally independent of any fossil fuel supply, but their output is intermittent, because the availability of solar energy during the day at a particular location is periodic in nature. Water pumping is one application of solar energy with great potential, since the complex problem of energy storage can be avoided by storing the pumped water. Most commercially available equipment converts solar radiation directly into electricity which powers an electric motor-driven pump.

Wind power As with solar power, the availability of wind energy at a particular site may vary considerably from day to day and with the seasons. Just as the economics of running an engine-driven pump will be closely tied to the cost of fuel, so the feasibility of wind pumps depends closely on the availability of wind energy. The energy in the wind is not directly proportional to its speed — in fact the output of a windmill varies with the cube of the wind-speed. In other words, doubling the wind-speed has the effect of increasing the available energy by a factor of eight ($2^3 = 8$), while a halving of the wind speed reduces the energy to one eighth. The energy availability being thus so much more variable than the wind speed means that it is generally not practicable to make use of winds with speeds lower than about 8 to 11km/h, while winds higher than about 50km/h tend to be too powerful to be used conveniently. It is important therefore that there are reasonably frequent winds available at a proposed windpump site in this range, preferably above 16km/h and certainly above 8km/h.

With greatly increased oil prices there is a considerable revival of interest in wind power both for water pumping and for electricity. The cattle- and sheep-raising industries of the arid central USA and central Australia still rely on water-pumping windmills in remote areas where fuel supplies or maintenance facilities are difficult to arrange for internal combustion engines. It has been estimated that as many as a million of these, mostly fitted to wells or boreholes, are in use around the world today. Windpumps are as yet not so widely used for irrigation, but notable examples from Crete and Peru demonstrate that under favourable conditions (low to medium lift) the use of many small locally manufactured machines can be a viable alternative to a single large windpump or other pumping system.

Diesel and petrol engines The internal combustion piston engine which, together with the electric motor, is by far the most common prime mover in the 5 to 500hp range, has developed in two main forms: the diesel (compression ignition) engine and the petrol (spark ignition) engine. The main reasons for the success of these engines is their convenient 'instant start' and 'independent run' capabilities, their compact size, their relatively high power-to-weight ratio and their cheapness. However, the internal combustion engine's main virtue is also its weakness, as in order to achieve easy combustion within the working cylinder it is necessary to use a clean and readily ignited fuel; they are therefore invariably dependent on petroleum-based fuels which have become increasingly expensive. In common with other complex machines they need regular maintenance to keep in satisfactory running order, and to achieve this a reliable supply of spare parts and lubricants will be essential, together with the relevant servicing skills.

When comparing different commercially available engines it soon becomes apparent that there is a tremendous variation in types available. Diesel engines tend to be heavier and are more robust in construction than petrol engines, which are more compact for their power output, and are simpler and cheaper to manufacture. The diesel engine is also inherently more efficient and often has a longer life and better reliability than the petrol equivalent. The main virtue of petrol engines is where light weight is needed, to allow easy portability, or where low capital cost and simplicity are important. It is a mistake however, in many cases, to consider capital cost as a primary choice criterion because the actual running costs depend at least as much on factors such as total engine life, fuel and maintenance costs. It follows from this that it is better to run an engine at a lower power than its 'maximum rated power' in order to prolong its life. Another reason for 'derating' is that better fuel economies can be obtained. For applications requiring continuous reliable operation for long periods, a large, heavy, slow-running engine would be a good choice, while for intermittent applications or where portability is needed, a cheap, compact high-speed machine may be appropriate.

Electric motors These are available in a very wide range of sizes from a fraction of a horsepower to over 100hp. They are generally more reliable than diesel and petrol engines and are, therefore, often preferred as a source of power for water pumps where a reliable supply of electricity is available. The electric motor should be capable of carrying the full load to be imposed on it, taking into consideration the various adverse operating conditions under which the pumping equipment may have to work. If the power requirement of the pump exceeds the safe operating load of the electric motor, the motor may be damaged or may even burn out. In the selection of motors for use in pumping systems, direct-current (d.c.) permanent-magnet motors are generally favoured, as these offer good efficiency even when operating under part-load conditions. Mass-produced alternating-current (a.c.) motors are only half as efficient as their d.c. equivalents. Moreover, they require an inverter (to convert d.c. to a.c.) implying a further loss in efficiency. Thus, the overall efficiency of a.c. electric motors is low. Conventional electric motors have a segmented commutator and brushes. As wear takes place new brushes are required — typically at intervals of about 2,000 to 4,000 hours of operation. If the brushes are not renewed when they are worn out the machine can be seriously damaged.

PORTABLE PUMPSETS

The majority of these consist of a self-priming centrifugal pump driven directly by internal combustion engine. The light-weight models are generally powered by 2- or 4-stroke petrol engines, the larger machines by diesel engine. The smallest pumpsets come fitted with a carrying handle or frame, while the bigger units are usually trolley- or skid-mounted.

'ALCON' MKIII CENTRIFUGAL PUMPSET A model (illustrated right) made of aluminium can be close couped to an electric motor or petrol engine. Capacities up to 30m³/h and maximum heads to 30m. A wide range of skid and trolley-mounted engine and motor-driven pumpsets is also available.

LA BOUR PUMP CO. LTD.
Denington Estate, Wellingborough
Northants, NN8 2QL
U.K.

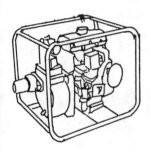

PORTABLE PUMP UNIT This steel bodied self-priming centrifugal pump, fitted with a pair of carrying handles, is available in two sizes, 51 and 76mm outlet diameter. Connected by belt-drive to a 5hp diesel or optional light-weight petrol engine, they have maximum outputs of approximately 30 and 70m³/h at an operating head of 9m. Weight 120kg.

ALVAN BLANCH DEV. CO. LTD.
Chelworth
Malmesbury, Wiltshire SN16 9SG
U.K.

CARPI B40 A self-priming centrifugal pump made of aluminium and close coupled to a 4hp 2-stroke petrol engine. Output 16m³/h at 5m total head or 1.6m³/h at 35m. Maximum suction head 7m.

F.LLI GIACOMO & LUIGI CARPI
42028 Poviglio, Reggio E
ITALY

DAE HEUNG WATER PUMPSET This

self-priming 76mm model weighing 35kg is mounted in a tubular carrying frame. Close coupled to a petrol engine, it has a maximum output of 66m³/h; maximum total head 15m. Belt-driven centrifugal pumps also available. Manufactured by Dae Heung Machinery Co. Ltd. and available from:

KOREA TRADE PROMOTION
CORPORATION
C.P.O. Box 1621, Seoul
KOREA

DANARM ENGINE PUMPS Model PE 25 weighing 10kg, is a 2hp 2-stroke, 25mm self-priming centrifugal pump set. Typical performance 3.5m³/h at 35m head. Maximum output 6.6m³/h; maximum total head 42m. A 5hp 4-stroke model is also available.

DANARM
Victoria Works
Birmingham Road, Dudley
West Midlands DY1 4RL
U.K.

'EASIPRIME' PUMPS Two basic self-priming 50mm models are available, the 4250 and 4256. They can be close coupled to a choice of power units — petrol, kerosene, and diesel engine or electric motor up to 2.2kW. Typical performance 15m³/h at 18m total head. 80 and 100mm sizes also available skid or trolley-mounted.

LEE HOWL PUMPS
Alexandra Road, Tipton
West Midlands DY4 8TA
U.K.

'TEXMO' SELF-PRIMING PUMPSET Available in two sizes, 51 and 63.5mm, close coupled to Enfield Villiers MK 12 and MK 25 petrol engines respectively. Weights 36 and 56kg.

THE ENFIELD INDIA LTD.
304 & 305 Anna Salai (Mount Road)
Madras 600 018
INDIA

'UNION' SP2 Similar to the Alcon model and powered by 2hp VIlliers petrol engine.

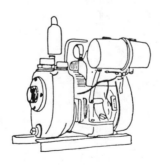

PULSA 3 HANDPUMP

This unusual new design uses rebound inertia to lift progressively an oscillating column of water. A piston and cylinder assembly at ground level are connected by a pressure hose to a submerged chamber fitted with a foot-valve and containing elastic elements. Lifts up to 50m. Output 8 litres/min.

FLUXINOS
Via Genoa 10, 58100 Grosseto
ITALY

ROWER PUMP

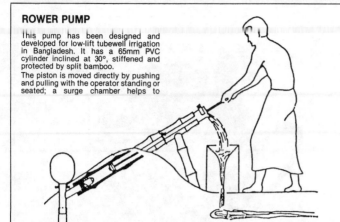

This pump has been designed and developed for low-lift tubewell irrigation in Bangladesh. It has a 65mm PVC cylinder inclined at 30°, stiffened and protected by split bamboo.

The piston is moved directly by pushing and pulling with the operator standing or seated; a surge chamber helps to improve operator comfort. Cheapness and ease of maintenance have been aimed for. The number of components have been reduced to a minimum and no special tools are needed for repairs. The piston and foot valve are easily removed by withdrawing them through the discharge opening. For protection the manufacturers recommend installing the pump partly buried in the ground so that only the discharge pipe is exposed. Suction lifts of up to 6m are possible but 2 to 4m is more typical. Output is in the order of 2 to 3m³/h, suitable for irrigating small plots. A household version is also available.

MIRPUR AGRICULTURAL WORKSHOP AND TRAINING SCHOOL (MAWTS)
Mirpur Section 12, Pallabi
Dhaka-16
BANGLADESH

AUTOMATIC HYDRAULIC RAM PUMPS

These are self-operating pumps with only two moving parts, in which the energy of a quantity of water with a small head is used to elevate a proportion to a higher level. Water flows from the source, which may be a flowing stream or spring, along the drive pipe and through the waste valve. The rapid flow of water through the open waste valve causes this to close suddenly and when this occurs the momentum of water in the drive pipe forces a proportion of the flow past the delivery valve, thus compressing the air in the pressure chamber and causing a continuous flow in the delivery pipe. If plenty of fall is available, hydrams can be worked by as little as 4 litres/min or if water is plentiful, falls as low as 0.6m can be used. They run continuously so long as the flow into the drive pipe is not interrupted.

Hydraulic ram pumps are manufactured in a variety of sizes to accommodate a range of falls and available flows. They generally have a low output and are best suited to domestic and livestock water supply, occasionally to small-scale irrigation.

The following examples illustrate the performance range of ram pumps. A 50mm model with a fall of 1m and a working flow of 1 litre/s can deliver 0.07 litre/s to a head of 10m or 0.22 litre/s to a head of 3m. A 100mm ram with a fall of 15m and a flow of 4.5 litres/s can deliver 0.5 litre/s to a head of 90m or 1.5 litres/s to a head of 30m.

BILLABONG HYDRAULIC RAM Available in six sizes with drive pipe diameters from 25 to 102mm and capacities from 0.05 to 2.25m³/h.

JOHN DANKS & SON PTY. LTD.
Doody Street, Alexandria
Sydney, N.S.W.
AUSTRALIA

GREEN & CARTER
Grange Farm, Northington
Alresford, Hants SO24 9TG,
U.K.

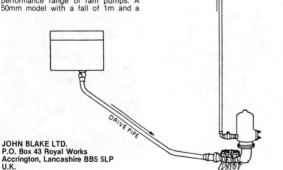

JOHN BLAKE LTD.
P.O. Box 43 Royal Works
Accrington, Lancashire BB5 5LP
U.K.

'MASTER' FADAMA PUMP

The 'Master' Fadama Pump illustrated above is a simple hand-operated piston type lift pump capable of raising approximately 8m³/h at a 1m lift or 5.5m³/h at a 3m. It operates equally well in clear or dirty water. The pump is supplied with either a baseplate for fixing to a hard standing or a tubular frame for free standing. Complete with 4m or 60mm suction hose, the package weighs 52k.

Another model, the 'Master' Mark 111 Pump is capable of raising approx. 10m³ at a 2m lift or 8m³ at 3 to 6m. A novel feature is a vacuum chamber incorporated into the wall of the pump which helps to eliminate surge and causes the water to flow smoothly. The pump is fully galvanized. Weight 82kg excluding hose.

L P ENGINEERING
Galloway Road
Bishop's Stortford, Herts
U.K.

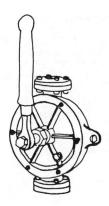

SEMI-ROTARY HANDPUMPS

This type of double-acting pump which is illustrated right, is commonly used for lifting small quantities of liquid and delivering it to a higher elevation. Typical applications are the filling of an overhead water tank from a lower source or the transfer of liquid fuels and oils from storage tank or barrel. The pump — sometimes known as a 'wing' pump — is operated by moving the handle from side to side in an arc of approximately 90 degrees. The cast iron body of the pump houses the semi-rotary pump mechanism which is fitted with brass or gun-metal flap valves.

Commonly available sizes are from 12.5 to 38mm (suction and delivery pipe diameters); up to 76mm occasionally available. Maximum suction lifts generally between 3 and 5m, delivery head 5 to 10m, and capacities from 15 to 150 litres/min. The fitting of non-return valves is sometimes suggested for the higher head installations.

A range of sizes are available from the following manufacturers:

PUMPENFABRIK BEYER
Dorfstraße 25, Ot Wulfsfelde
2361 Pronstorf
W. GERMANY

CENTRAL INDIA ENGINEERING CO.
2153/5 Hill Street, Ranigunj
Secunderabad 500 003 A.P.
INDIA

FABRICA DE IMPLEMENTOS
AGRICOLAS (FIASA)
Hortiguera 1882, 1406 Buenos Aires
ARGENTINA

POMPES GRILLOT
Rue de l'Observance
B.P. 118, 84007 Avignon
FRANCE

RENSON ET CIE
BP 23, 59550 Landrecies
FRANCE

WIND-POWERED PUMPS

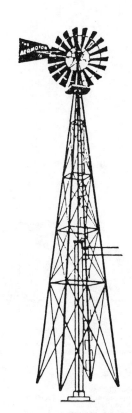

In general, water pumping windmills have multi-bladed rotors. The reason for this is that a high starting torque is needed to get a water pump started, and the provision of many blades eases starting against a heavy load in light winds. Also multi-bladed rotors run slowly in a given wind which makes this design the natural choice for connecting to reciprocating piston pumps which need to be operated at quite low speeds.

The performance of a windpump is sensitive to the size of pump fitted — fitting a smaller pump will allow the windmill to start in a lower windspeed than a bigger pump. Good judgement is required to fit a pump which will maximise the output from the machine in a given wind regime.

Typical performance figures for a 4.9m diameter windpump are given in the table below.

Wind speed km/h	Head × Output m.m³/h
8	61
16	122
24	183
32	244
40	305

Most machines are designed to make use of windspeeds between 8 and 50km/h. They do not function in lower windspeeds and invariably either furl themselves or deliberately shed a lot of the available power at higher windspeeds with the aid of an automatic governing or furling system to prevent any damage.

The three main uses for windpumps are livestock water supplies, village water supplies and irrigation. Water for the latter is characterized by a large variation in requirements from month to month and in order to satisfy peak demand generally it is only economic to lift from shallow depths. Due to the variability of wind, if a supply of water must be guaranteed, it will be necessary either to provide storage or a standby capability.

MULTI-BLADED WINDPUMPS

The following manufacturers make multi-bladed 'American' type windpumps. An asterisk(*) indicates machines greater than 5m diameter available. The list is adapted from a Technical Brief prepared by IT Power Ltd; it is for general information only and inclusion of any product does not infer that it is specifically recommended.

Illustrated left is a typical example of a multi-bladed windpump. Illustrated right is the Kijito windpump manufactured by Bobs Harries Engineering Ltd. of Kenya.

DEMPSTER INDUSTRIES INC.*
P.O. Box 848
Beatrice, Nebraska 68310
U.S.A.

FIASA
Hortiguera 1882, 1406 Buenos Aires
ARGENTINA

S.A. GUILLEMINOT
Place de l'Eglise
10270 Lusigny-sur-Barse
FRANCE

ALSTHOM ATLANTIQUE*
18320 Jouet sur l'Aubois
FRANCE

ALSTON WINDMILLS PTY. LTD.
Branthorne Street
Gisborne, Victoria
AUSTRALIA

HELLER ALLER CO. INC.
P.O. Box 29
Corner Perry 7 Oakwood Streets
Napoleon, Ohio 43545
U.S.A.

CLIMAX, WYATT BRO. (WHITCHURCH) LTD.
Wayland Works
Whitchurch, Salop SY13 1RS
U.K.

'COMET', SIDNEY WILLIAMS & CO. LTD.*
P.O. Box 22, Dulwich Hill, NSW 2203
AUSTRALIA

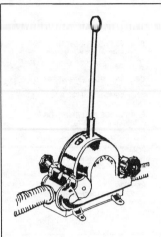

DIAPHRAGM HANDPUMPS

The self priming pumps are particularly useful for moving water containing suspended solids. Generally small and light-weight, they can be supplied with flexible suction and delivery hoses for transportation. Double-acting models — an example is shown left — have twin diaphragms usually made of nitrite or butyl rubber and are easily accessible when replacement becomes necessary. Maximum suction lift is normally between 4 and 7m, delivery head from 2 to 5m, and output from 60 to 140 litres/min. Typical applications are: dewatering on construction sites; bilge and barrel emptying; and drinking water supplies.

The following make a range of both single and double-acting diaphragm handpumps.

PUMPENFABRIK BEYER
Dorfstraße 25, Ot Wulfsfelde
2361 Pronstorf
W. GERMANY

PATAY PUMPS LTD.
The Ridgeway, Iver, Bucks.
U.K.

Heavier duty hand-operated diaphragm pumps designed for agricultural purposes and capable of delivery heads of up to 12m have outputs from 80 to 120 litres/min. Illustrated right, these can also be trolley mounted for easier transportation.

POMPES GRILLOT
Rue de l'Observance
B.P. 118, 84007 Avignon
FRANCE

RENSON ET CIE
BP 23, 59550 Landrecies
FRANCE

'CONTRACTOR'S' DIAPHRAGM PUMPS

Model No. 2745 is a lift-only pump suitable for raising large quantities of water containing sand, grit or sewage. Four sizes available with optional double actuating hand levers. Capacities from 90 to 450 litres/min. Lift and force model No. 2746 also available.

HATTERSLEY NEWMAN HENDER LTD.
Burscough Road, Ormskirk
Lancashire L39 2XG
U.K.

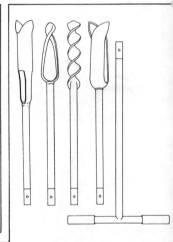

SOIL SURVEYING AND DRILLING

The following type of equipment is available from this manufacturer for soil research and shallow wells and latrine construction, and surveying. They also supply a range of instruments for hydrogeological, meteorological and agricultural research.

HAND AUGERS A full range of augers is available for investigations up to 7m in depth. An example is illustrated left.

BAILER BORING EQUIPMENT Tripods, winches and bailer boring rig for performing augerings down to 15m. Not for use in hard or stony soils. Use of steel casings allows depths of 25m to be reached.

MOTORIZED SOIL AUGER This machine can be used for general soil research and for drilling holes for posts, tree planting or vertical drainage. Uses half-flighted augers of 50 to 500mm diameter.

SHALLOW WELLS SURVEY SET Hand-operated auger set for determining the presence of water in the subsoil in order to assist choice of potential well sites. Suitable for investigations up to 20m.

SHALLOW WELLS CONSTRUCTION SET Light and heavy (shown above) hand-drilling sets available for use in soils without very hard layers and with sufficient aquifer recharge to permit small-diameter wells. Standard set equipped with 165 × 150mm casing; heavy set with 220 × 200mm. Maximum depth approximately 20m.

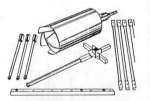

LATRINE DRILLING SET Shown above, the light set can be used to make holes of 250mm diameter and up to 10m deep for sanitation purposes. Heavy set available for 400mm holes.

SURVEYING INSTRUMENTS: including Abney levels, clinometers.

EIJKELKAMP
Equipment for Soil Research B.V.
Nijverheidsstraat 14
6987 EM Giesbeek
NETHERLANDS

SOLAR-POWERED PUMPS

There are two methods by which solar energy can be converted to mechanical energy for water pumping; direct conversion of solar radiation to electricity by an array of photovoltaic (PV) cells and then to mechanical energy by an electric motor; or conversion of solar energy to heat which can then be used to drive a thermal heat engine. At present, the former system appears to be the more promising, although a major drawback is its high capital cost.

The main components of a PV system are illustrated in the figure below which shows a submerged motor-pump set installed in a borehole. The array at ground level is connected by electric cable to the motor which drives the pump directly. On the right is shown an alternative installation using a submerged pump coupled by drive shaft to a surface-mounted electric motor. Other components which may be incorporated in the system between the array and the motor are an electronic control system, a battery and an inverter. Provision for water storage may also be desirable.

The following list prepared by IT Power Ltd. is for information only and does not imply any recommendation or endorsement of the products of any of the suppliers included.

SOLAPAK LTD.
Factory 3, Lock Lane
High Wycombe
U.K.

PHOTOWATT INTERNATIONAL SA
98 ter blvd. Heloise
95102 Argenteuil
FRANCE

B.P. SOLAR SYSTEMS LTD.
Aylesbury Vale Industrial Park
Farmborough Close, Stocklake
Aylesbury, Bucks HP20 1DQ
U.K.

AEG TELEFUNKEN
Industriestraße 29, 200 Wedel
W. GERMANY

ANSALDO (SOCIETA GENERALE ELETTROMECCANICA SpA)
via Nicola Lorenzzi 8
16152 Genova, Cornigliano
ITALY

ARCO SOLAR INC.
20554 Plummer Street, Chatsworth
California 91311
U.S.A.

BRIAU S.A.
BP 43
37009 Tours Cedex
FRANCE

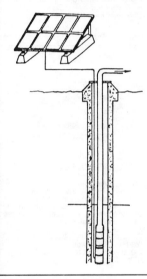

FLYWHEEL ASSISTED LIFT-AND-FORCE PUMPS

On the Godwin Series X, a heavy duty, mainly cast iron, double flywheel model, reciprocating motion is achieved by twin connecting rods and crosshead. Fitted with balance weights, the handwheels are extra wide for optional belt drive. Extractable or non-extractable cylinders available in eight sizes from 57 to 102mm for matching maximum heads from 53 to 12m. Corresponding outputs 13 and 41 litres/min at 40 strokes, the former with two operators.

H.J. GODWIN LTD.
Quenington, Circencester
Glos. GL7 5BY
U.K.

BARNABY CLIMAX LIFT AND FORCE PUMP Similar to the Godwin Series X. Lubrication of the crankshaft ball bearings is by a force fed self-oiling system.

BARNABY CLIMAX
White Ladies Close
Little London, Worcester WR1 1PZ
U.K.

WELL POINTS

Under favourable soil conditions well points (above left) can be driven into the ground on the end of a length of piping and a pump attached for extracting ground-water. The point is usually made from heavy-duty solid cast iron or forged steel and the strainer through which water enters the perforated pipe section during pumping is made from brass.

FOOTVALVES AND STRAINERS

Fitted at the base of rising mains and pump inlets these are usually designed to be non-clogging or self-cleaning. They are typically made from cast iron with bronze internal parts. Illustrated below left. Available from the following manufacturers, the first three of which also supply well points:

PUMPENFABRIK BEYER
Dorfstraße 25, Ot Wulfsfelde
2361 Pronstorf
W. GERMANY

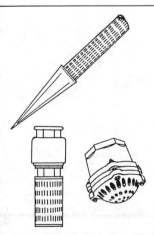

CENTRAL INDIA ENGINEERING CO.
2153/5 Hill Street, Ranigunj
Secunderabad 500 003 A.P.
INDIA

BARNABY CLIMAX
White Ladies Close
Little London, Worcester WR1 1PZ
U.K.

DUNWELL PRODUCTS
P.O. Box 8543, Belmont
Bulawayo
ZIMBABWE

HATTERSLEY NEWMAN HENDER LTD.
Burscough Road, Ormskirk
Lancashire L39 2XG
U.K.

KUMAR INDUSTRIES
Edathara Post 678 611, Palghat District
Kerala
INDIA

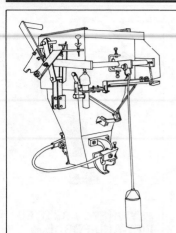

AUTOMATIC BAGGER AND WEIGHER

Oriental Workshops produce 3 models of this machine which automatically bags and weighs farm produce such as grain. It is able to handle loads of 1-15 kg (Precision model), 5-50 kg (Master model) and 10-100 kg (Super model) with an accuracy of ±0.1%.

The bagging and weighing process is achieved through a balance assembly which is controlled by a piston set in an oil bath. The piston movements are damped by a rod and rocker mechanism which minimizes oscillations of the balance and speeds up the bag-filling operation.

ORIENTAL SCIENCE APPARATUS WORKSHOPS
Jawaharlal Nehru Marg
Cantt — 133001, Haryana
INDIA

FENCING PLIERS

This multipurpose fencing tool acts as a plier, hammer, wire cutter and strainer, and removes staples and nails. It is supplied by:

DALTON SUPPLIES LTD.
Nettlebed
Henley-on-Thames RG9 5AB, Oxon
U.K.

SELF SUFFICIENCY AND SMALLHOLDING SUPPLIES
Little Burcott, Wells
Somerset BA5 1NQ
U.K.

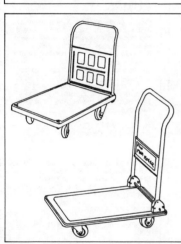

HAND TRUCKS

Although less robust than the sack and case trucks, this type of hand cart is able to handle bulkier loads. This is afforded by the larger loading pallet to which 2 swivel (front) and 2 rigid (back) casters are fitted. The casters give the truck a good manoeuvrability even when carrying capacity loads (120-500 kg according to model and manufacturer).

COSMO INCORPORATED
Towa Bldg 4th Floor
10,4 — Chome, Awaji-Machi
Higashi-Ku, Osaka
JAPAN

J.J. BLOW LTD.
Oldfield Works, Chatsworth Road
Chesterfield S40 2DJ
U.K.

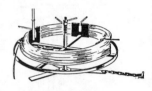

WIRE DISPENSER

Fencing wire may be dispensed from reels such as the one illustrated above. This dispenser is suitable for running out all sizes of wire. It is secured in the ground by means of a central stake and has a spring tension brake.

ERNEST HAYES (NZ) LTD.
789 Main South Road
P.O. Box 23042, Christchurch 4
NEW ZEALAND

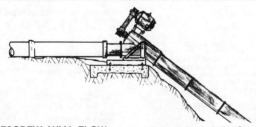

BATESCREW AXIAL FLOW PUMPS

These low-lift high discharge pumps can be powered by electric motor, diesel or petrol engine connected directly or by belt-drive. They consist of a shaft-driven axial flow impeller mounted at the lower end of the discharge pipe. Installation can be either vertical or at an angle as illustrated. Available in a range of sizes, the smallest powered by a 3hp motor has a capacity of approximately 300m³/h at 1m head. Alternatively a 9hp model can deliver 330m³/h at a total head of 4.6m or 950m³/h at 1m.

Portable 3.5 and 5hp models also available driven by 2-stroke and 4-stroke petrol engines. Typical performance 120m³/h at 1m.

BATESCREW ENGINEERING PTY. LTD.
Deniliquin Street
Tocumwal N.S.W. 2714
AUSTRALIA

PUMP ACCESSORIES

Most manufacturers should be able to supply spares for their particular pump models. Usually these will be the wearing parts such as cup washers for reciprocating piston pumps, shown below, and other valve components. Some will also provide individual pump parts such as the pump cylinder assembly shown above, cylinder cap gaskets, spool and ball valves, or the basic pump stand.

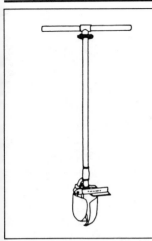

EARTH AUGERS

The earth auger (pictured left) has cutting edges of high carbon steel. It is adjustable to bore holes of 150mm to 400mm diameter, for the purpose of preparing fence post holes.

KUMAON NURSERY
Ramnagar — 244715
Nainital, U.P.
INDIA

Earth augers are also supplied by:

GUTHRIE TRADING PTY.
240 Currie Street
Adelaide, SA 5001
AUSTRALIA

SEYMOUR MAN. CO. INC.
500 North Broadway, P.O. Box 248
Seymour, Indiana 47274
U.S.A.

MAWROB CO. (ENGINEERS) LTD.
121a/125a Sefton Street
Southport, Merseyside PR8 5DR
U.K.

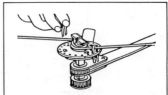

WIRE TIGHTENER

Tighteners of the type illustrated above which are used with detachable handles may be obtained from:

RANCHMAN INDUSTRIES LTD.
P.O. Box 8321, Riccarton
Christchurch
NEW ZEALAND

WELBY-EZY-WAY PRODUCTS LTD.
25 Morgan Street, Newmarket
Auckland
NEW ZEALAND

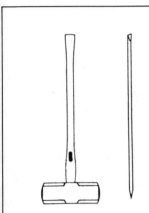

SLEDGE HAMMER AND CROWBAR

Tools of this type for driving posts and making holes are supplied by:

BULLDOG TOOLS
Clarington Forge, Wigan
Lancashire WN1 3DD
U.K.

LEON CLEMENT & CIE
Corravillers
70310 Faucogney (Haute-Saône)
FRANCE

BULAWAYO STEEL PRODUCTS
8 Ironbridge Road, Donnington
P.O. Box 1603, Bulawayo
ZIMBABWE

TROPIC
B.P. 706, Douala
CAMEROON

EDELMIRO VAZQUEZ Y HNO., S.L.
Apartado 64, Avenida de Vigo 126
Pontevedra
SPAIN

WIRE STRAINERS

Chain wire strainers with wire splicing tool of the type illustrated above are available from:

ELIZA TINSLEY & CO. LTD.
P.O. Box 35, Reddal Hill Road
Cradley Heath, Warley
W. Midlands B64 5JF
U.K.

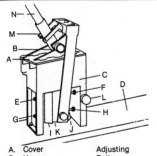

CINVA-RAM BLOCK PRESS

The CINVA-Ram Block Press is a simple, low-cost portable machine for making building blocks and tiles from common soil. The press, made entirely of steel, has a mould box in which a hand-operated piston compresses a slightly moistened mixture of soil and cement or lime. Bearing strength (Fully cured blocks): 14-35 kg/cm$_3$.
   Size of block: 9 cm × 14 cm × 29 cm.
   Average number of blocks per 100 lbs of cement: 150.
   Among many manufacturers it is available from:

BELLOW'S VALVAIR INTERNATIONAL
200 W. Exchange St.
Akron, Ohio 44309
U.S.A.

METALIBEC LTDA.
Apartado Aereo 233 NAL 157
Bucaramanga
COLOMBIA

A. Cover
B. Upper Saddle
C. Mold Box
D. Baseboard
E. & F. Upper Adjusting Bolts
G. & H. Lower Adjusting Bolts
I. & J. Guide Plates
K. Piston
L. Lower Rollers
M. Lever Latch
N. Handle

POST DRIVER

This implement consists of a heavy tube, with its upper end closed, and two handles. The tube is placed over the post, and used instead of a mallet or sledge hammer. The implement is easy to use and does not damage the heads of the posts.
   Post drivers of this design are available from:

DRIVALL LTD.
Churchbridge Works, Cannock
Staffordshire WS11 3JP
U.K.

MAWROB CO. (ENGINEERS) LTD.
121a/125a Sefton Street
Southport, Merseyside PR8 5DR
U.K.

DONALD PRESSES LTD.
P.O. Box 138, Masterton
NEW ZEALAND

Appendix 2
Manufacturers' Index

Argentina

FÁBRICA DE IMPLEMENTOS AGRÍCOLAS (FIASA)
Hortiguera 1882
1406 Buenos Aires
Tel: 923-1055
Telex: 22910 CAMEX AR

Australia

ALSTON WINDMILLS PTY. LTD
Branthorne Street
Gisborne
Victoria

BATESCREW ENGINEERING PTY. LTD.
Deniliquin Street
Tocumwal
N.S.W. 2714
Tel: TOCUMWAL 101 & 281
Telex: AA 56087

BORAL CYCLONE LTD
221-223 East Boundary Road
P.O Box 77
East Bentleigh
Victoria 3165
Tel: 579-1777
Telex: AA 36016
Cable: SCREENWIRE MELBOURNE

'COMET' SIDNEY WILLIAMS & CO. LTD
P.O Box 22
Dulwich Hill
N.S.W. 2203

DANKS, JOHN & SON, PTY. LTD
Doody Street
Alexandria
Sydney
N.S.W.

GUTHRIE TRADING PTY
240 Currie Street
Adelaide
S.A. 5001

Austria

REFORM-WERKE BAUER & CO. GmbH
Postfach 192
Haidestraße 40
4600 Wels
Tel: (07242) 7377
Telex: 025539
Cable: REFORMWERKE WELS

Bangladesh

MIRPUR AGRICULTURAL WORKSHOP & TRAINING SCHOOL (MAWTS)
Mirpur Section 12
Pallabi
Dhaka 16

Belgium

ASE EUROPE N.V.
Century Centre
de-Keyserlei, 58 Box 1
2018 Antwerp
Tel: (032) 34 06 66
Telex: 31143 ACMET B
Cable: ASEUROP FODDERS ANTWERP

Brazil

IRMAOS NOGUEIRA S.A.
Rua XV de Novembro, 781
13970. — 1 Itapira
Sao Paulo
Tel: (0192) 63-1500
Telex: (019) 2380 INOG BR

KNUPP SCHIER, & CIA LTDA
Rua Bento Gonçalves, 3030
93.300 Novo Hamburgo, (R.S.)
Tel: 93-6277
Telex: 512884 MOOR BR Att. KRUPP
Cable: KRUPP

PONTAL MATERIAL RODANTE S.A.
Rua Campante No. 237, Vila Independência
Caixa Postal 8333
01.000 Sao Paulo, (S.P.)

Cameroon

TROPIC
BP 706
Douala
Tel: 42-42-56
Telex: TROPIC 5316 KN DOUALA
Cable: TLX TROPIC-DOUALA

China

CHINA NATIONAL AGRICULTURAL MACHINERY, IMPORT AND EXPORT CORPORATION
26 South Yeutan Street
Beijing
Tel: 866361
Telex: 22467 AMPRC CN
Cable: AGRIMEX

Colombia

METALIBEC LTDA
Apartado Aereo 233-Nal 157
Bucaramanga

Denmark

HANSEN COMP, A.B.C., A/S
Hauchsvej 14
Postbus 3054
1508 Copenhagen V
Tel: (1) 316806
Telex: 15496 ABCH DK

PRESIDENT MØLLERIMASKINER A/S
4300 Holbaek
Tel: (03) 430111
Telex: 44153
Cable: PRESIDENT

France

ALSTHOM ATLANTIQUE
18320 Jouet sur l'Aubois
Tel: (48) 76.40.14

BELIN INTERNATIONAL
2 Mail des Charmilles
BP 194
10006 Troyes Cedex
Tel: (25) 72.41.66
Telex: 840 559F

BOURGUIGNON, S.C.A.D.
BP 17
26301 Bourg-de-Péage-Cedex
Drome
Tel: (75) 70.23.85
Telex: 345 951F

BRIAU S.A.
BP 43
37009 Tours Cedex
Tel: (47) 61.38.17
Telex: 750 729F

CLÉMONT, LÉON, & CIE
Corravillers
70310 Faucogney (Haute-Saône)
Tel: (84) 94.40.28
Telex: CLEMENT 362 808F
Cable: CLEMENT CORRAVILLERS

COMIA-FAO, STE., S.A.
27 Blvd. de Châteaubriant
BP 91
35500 Vitré
Tel: (99) 75.20.97
Telex: 950 457F

E.B.R.A.28 rue du Maine
BP 915
49009 Angers Cedex
Tel: (41) 43.23.00
Telex: EBRA 720 348F

ELECTRA
47170 Poudenas
Tel: (58) 65.73.55/65.70.22
Telex: 541 085 ELECTRA

GAUBERT, A., ETS
22 rue Gambetta
BP 24
16700 Ruffec
Tel: (45) 31.00.86/31.01.07
Telex: PAR 791020 PUBLIC ANGONLEME F

GUILLEMINOT, S.A.
Place de l'Elise
19270 Lusigny-sur-Barse
Tel: (25) 45.22.26

MANUFACTURE FRANÇAISE DE FOURCHES
3 rue de Lyon
Terrenoire
BP 4
42011 Saint-Etienne Cedex
Tel: (77) 53.71.55
Telex: ITASE 370 425F

TOOLS FOR ORGANIC FARMING

MARPEX
1 rue Thurot
4000 Nantes

OUTILS WOLF
Rue de l'Industrie
67160 Wissembourg
Tel: (88) 94.14.99
Telex: 870815

PHOTOWATT INTERNATIONAL S.A.
98 ter blvd. Heloise
95102 Argenteuil

POMPES GRILLOT
Rue de l'Observance
BP 118
84007 Avignon
Tel: (90) 81.02.12

RENSON & CIE
BP 23
59550 Landrecies
Tel: (27) 84.71.77
Telex: 820705 RENSON LANDR
Cable: RENSON LANDRECIES

S.A.M.A.P.
1 rue du Molin
Andolsheim
BP 1
68600 Neuf-Brisach
Tel: (85) 71.46.36

S.E.C.A.
38260 La Côte St. André
Tel: (74) 20.48.19
Telex: 340396 CHAMCO PR SECA

TÉCHINÉ, ETS
82400 Valence d'Agen (T&G)
Tel: (63) 39.50.31

India

**AMAR AGRICULTURAL IMPLEMENTS
WORKS**
Amar Street
Gill Road
Janta Nagar
Ludhiana 141 003
Tel: 28985/27423
Cable: IMPLEMENTS (M)

**ANDHRA PRADESH AGRICULTURAL
UNIVERSITY**
Rajendranagar
Hyderabad 500 030

CENTRAL INDIA ENGINEERING CO
2153/5 Hill Street
Ranigunj
Secunderabad 500 003 A.P.
Tel: 76831
Cable: CIECO

COSSUL & CO. PVT. LTD
123/367 — Industrial Area
Fazalgunj
Kanpur U.P.
Tel: 21020
Telex: 0325-309 COSL
Cable: IMPLEMENTS

**DANDEKAR BROTHERS (ENGINEERS &
FOUNDERS)**
Shivaji Nagar
Sangli
Maharashtra 416 416
Tel: 2299
Cable: DANDEKAR BROS

ENFIELD INDIA LTD
304-305 Anna Salai (Mount Road)
Madras 600 018
Tel: 110177
Telex: 041 231 (NFLD-IN)
Cable: GENGLYDE, MADRAS

HINDSONS PVT. LTD
The Lower Mall
Patiala 147 001
Punjab
Tel: 4238

KISAN KRISHI YANTRA UDYOG
64 Moti Bhawan
Collectorganj
Kanpur 208 001
Tel: 68945
Cable: GRIHLAXMI

KUMAON NURSERY
Ramnagar 244 715
Nainital U.P.
Tel: 39
Cable: NURSERY

**MAHARASHTRA AGRO. IND. DEV.
CORPORATION LTD**
Rajan House, 3rd Floor
Near Century Bazar
Prabhadevi
Bombay 400 025
Tel: 458211
Cable: KRUSHIUDYOG

**THE ORIENTAL SCIENCE APPARATUS
WORKSHOPS**
Jawaharlal Nehru Marg
Cantt 133 001
Haryana
Tel: 20796
Telex: 392-204 OSAWIN
Cable: SCIENCE

**RAJAN UNIVERSAL EXPORTS (MFRS.)
PVT. LTD**
P.O Box 250
Madras 600 001
Tel: 27552
Telex: 41-7587 RAJA IN
Cable: BIMLAEX

UNION FORGINGS
Focal Point
Sherpur
Ludhiana
Punjab
Tel: 23636

VICON LTD
K.R. Puram-Whitefield Road
Mahadevapura Post
Bangalore 560 048
Karnataka
Tel: Whitefield 217
Cable: VICONTACT — BANGALORE
Telex: 0845 316

Israel

B.F. EQUIPMENT
30080 Sde Yaakov
Tel: (04) 932636
Telex: 46400 BXHA-IL Ext 8067

KISLUK, A
Industrial Zone
P.O. Box 195
Afula Elit 18101
Tel: (065) 923767
Telex: 45181 ARAN IL ATTN KISLUK 144

**TECHNOHAC AGRICULTURAL
MACHINERY & IMPLEMENTS LTD**
New Industry Region
P.O. Box 660
Petakh-Tikva
Tel: 921198
Telex: 341118-9 FOT 5270
Cable: TECHNOHAC PETAKH TIKVA

YODLA, DOV & SONS
P.O. Box 246
Givatayim 53102
Tel: (03) 960234/5
Telex: 34118 BXTV IL Ext 5932

Italy

ALPINA
31015 Conegliano
Treviso
Tel: (0438) 40141
Telex: 410567 ITALY

**ANSALDO (SOCIETA GENERALE
ELETTROMECCANICA) SpA**
Via Nicola Lorenzzi 8
16152 Genova
Comigliano

BARBIERI SpA
Via Circonvallazione 19
36040 Sossano
Vicenza
Tel: (0444) 885239
Telex: 480609 BF SPA I

BERTOLINI MACCHINE AGRICOLE SpA
Via Guicciardi 7
42100 Reggio Emilia
Tel: (0522) 91000
Telex: 530662 BERMA I

CARPI, F.LLI GIACOMO & LUIGI
42028 Poviglio
Via Romana 82-R.E.
Tel: (0522) 68 97 41
Telex: 530279 CARPI I

FERRARI, O.M. SpA
Via Valbrina 19
42045 Luzzara (RE)
Tel: (0522) 835524
Telex: 530144 FERMAC I

FLUXINOS
Apparecchiature dei Fluidi
Via Genoa 10
58100 Grosseto
Tel: (0564) 451272

M.A.B. DI GUIDO BOCCHINI
Via Erbosa
47030 Gatteo (FO)
Tel: (0541) 930404
Telex: 550884 MABAGRI

NARDI FRANCESCO & FIGLI
06017 Selci Lama
Perugia
Tel: (075) 8582180
Telex: 660074 NARDI I
Cable: NARDI/LAMA/PERUGIA

Japan

COSMO INCORPORATED
Towa Bld. 4th Floor
10 Awaji-Machi 4-chome
Higashi-Ku
Osaka

Tel: 227-0707
Telex: COSMO J 64568
Cable: COSMOINCORP OSAKA

**SUZUE AGRICULTURAL MACHINERY
   CO. LTD**
144-2 Gomen-cho
Nankoku-Shi
Kochi-Ken 783
Tel: (06) 541-5121
Telex: J63115 NISTX

YAMAMOTO MFG. CO. LTD
813-17 Tendo-Ko
Tendo-Shi
Yamagata Ken 994
Tel: Tendo (02365) 3-3411
Telex: 8722 66 YMCTND J
Cable: YAMAMOTOTENDO. YAMAGATA

Kenya

NDUME PRODUCTS LTD
P.O. Box 62
Gilgil
Tel: 245
Telex: 39801 GILGIL

Korea

**KOREA TRADE PROMOTION
   CORPORATION**
C.P.O. Box 1621
Seoul
Tel: 753-4180/9
Telex: KOTRA K23659 K27326
Cable: KOTRA SEOUL

Netherlands

EIJKELKAMP
Equipment for Soil Research BR
Nijverheidsstraat 14
6987 EM Giesbeek
Tel: 08336-1941
Telex: 35416 EYKEL NL
Cable: EYKELSOIL LATHUM

RUMPSTAD BV
Postbus 1
3243 ZD Stan Aan't-Haringvliet
Tel: 01871-1202
Telex: 22585

TRAAS METAL BV
Groene Kruisstraat 3
4414 AL Waarde (2)

New Zealand

DONALD PRESSES LTD
P.O. Box 138
Masterton

HAYES, ERNEST, (NZ) LTD
P.O. Box 23042
789 Main South Road
Christchurch 4
Telex: 4415

RANCHMAN INDUSTRIES LTD
P.O. Box 8321 Riccarton
Christchurch
Tel: (03) 382-735

WELBY-EZY-WAY PRODUCTS LTD
25 Morgan Street
Newmarket
Aukland
Tel: 796-438

Nigeria

**E.L.A. AGRIC. MACHINERY MFG. &
   ENGINEERING CO**
E9/914B Iwo Road
Ibadan

Norway

ELKEM A/S
Christiania Spigerverk
P.O. Box 4224
Torshov
Oslo 4
Tel: (02) 234090
Telex: 71131

LIEN, K.K., FABRIKK A/S
Tromøy, Arendal
4812 Kongshamn
Tel: (041) 88100
Cable: PLOGFABRIKK

Philippines

JCCE INDUSTRIES
242 Mayondon
Los Baños
Laguna
Tel: 50011
Cable: JCCE, COLLEGE, LAGUNA, PHIL

KAUNLARAN INDUSTRIES
Calamba
Laguna

MBP ENGINEERING
K.M. 16 MacArthur Highway
Malanday
Valenzuela
Metro Manila

POYING'S WELDING SHOP
262 National Hi-Way
Brgy. Anos
Los Baños
Laguna
Tel: 831 9086
Telex: 63199 ETPI MO PN
Cable: POYINGWELD MANILA

Poland

AGROMET MOTOIMPORT
P.O. Box 900
Warsaw
Tel: 28-5071
Telex: 813665
Cable: MOTORIM

Portugal

COMPANHIA INDUSTRIAL DE FUNDICAO
17 Rue de Sao Joao 27
4000 Porto
Tel: 24927
Cable: ARADOS

Spain

EDELMIRO VAZQUEZ Y HNO. S.L.
Apartado 64
Avenida de Vigo 126
Pontevedra
Tel: (986) 85 99 61/85 20 65

Sri Lanka

MAHINDRA ENTERPRISES
507 Prince of Wales Avenue
Colombo 14
Tel: 32410
Cable: SWIGSON

Thailand

CHAIPRADIT KARNCHANG
235 Moo 8 Chiang Mai-Hang Dong Road
A-Hang Dong
Chiang Mai

United Kingdom

AL-KO BRITAIN LTD
No.1 Industrial Estate
Medomsley Road
Consett
County Durham DH8 6SZ
Tel: (0207) 590295
Telex: 538203 ALKO UK G

**ALVAN BLANCH DEVELOPMENT CO.
   LTD**
Chelworth
Malmesbury
Wilts SN16 9SG
Tel: (06667) 333
Telex: ALVAN B G 44304

ARNOLDS VETERINARY PRODUCTS LTD
14 Tessa Road
Richfield Avenue
Reading
Berks RG1 8NF
Tel: (0734) 54064
Telex: 847465 ARNVET G

BLAIR ENG. LTD
Rattray
Blairgowrie PH10 7DN
Scotland
Tel: (0250) 2244
Telex: 76243

B.P. SOLAR SYSTEMS LTD
Aylesbury Vale Ind. Park
Farnborough Close
Stocklake
Aylesbury
Bucks HP20 1DQ
Tel: 0296 26100
Telex: 838867

BARNABY CLIMAX LTD
White Ladies Close
Little London
Worcester WR1 1PZ

BENTALL SIMPLEX LTD
P.O. Box 10
Normanby Park
Industrial Estate
Scunthorpe
South Humberside DN15 8QW
Tel: 0724 282928
Telex: 99261 BETAL G

TOOLS FOR ORGANIC FARMING

BLOW, J.J., LTD
Oldfield Works
Chatsworth Road
Chesterfield S40 2DJ
Tel: (0246) 76635
Telex: 54598

BULLDOG TOOLS
Clarington Forge
Wigan
Lancashire WN1 3DD
Tel: (0942) 44281
Telex: 67325

CARTHORSE CO. LTD
Egremont Farm
Payhembury
Honiton
Devon EX14 0JA
Tel: (040 484) 233

CHRISTY & NORRIS LTD
Kings Road
Chelmsford
Essex CM1 1SA
Tel: (0245) 264077
Telex: 99266

COX, ALFRED, (SURGICAL) LTD
Edward Road
Coulsdon
Surrey CR3 2XA
Tel: 01-668 2131

DALTON SUPPLIES LTD
Nettlebed
Henley-on-Thames
Oxon RG9 5AB
Tel: (0491) 641457
Telex: 847547
Cable: ROTOTAG HENLEY-ON-THAMES
(UK)

DANARM LTD
Victoria Works
Birmingham Road
Dudley
West Midlands DY1 4RL
Tel: (0384) 455461
Telex: 336170 GILLOT G

DRIVALL LTD
Churchbridge Works
Cannock
Staffordshire WS11 3JP
Tel: (0922) 414288
Telex: 338327 GILPIN G
Cable: DRIVALL CANNOCK

FLOWSOW ENGINEERING CO
Slides
Silverhill
Robertsbridge
Sussex TN32 5PA
Tel: (0580) 880786

**GEEST OVERSEAS MECHANISATION
LTD**
Marsh Lane
Boston
Lincolnshire PE21 7RP
Tel: (0205) 69019
Telex: 32494

GODWIN, H.J. LTD
Quenington
Cirencester
Glos GL7 5BY
Tel: (028 575) 271
Telex: 43240
Cable: PUMPS CIREN

GREEN & CARTER
Grange Farm
Northington
Alresford
Hants SO24 9TG
Tel: (096 273) 2168

HATTERSLEY NEWMAN HENDER LTD
Burscough Road
Ormskirk
Lancashire L39 2XG
Tel: (0695) 77195
Telex: 62571
Cable: VALVES ORMSKIRK

HONDA U.K. LTD
Power Road
Chiswick W4 5YT
Tel: 01-747 1400
Telex: 28612

HUNT, R., & CO. LTD
52 High Street
Earls Coon
Colchester
Essex
Tel: (078 75) 2032
Telex: 98285
Cable: HUNT EARLS COLNE

JALO ENGINEERING LTD
Wimborne Industrial Estate
Mill Lane
Wimborne
Dorset
Tel: (0202) 885079

KONGSKILDE U.K. LTD
Holt
Norfolk NR25 6EE
Tel: (026 371) 3291
Telex: 97425
Cable: KOMAS
Telex: HOLT, NORFOLK

L.P. ENGINEERING
Galloway Road
Bishop's Stortford
Herts
Tel: (0279) 57713
Telex: 81674 BISS G

LA BOUR PUMP CO
Denington Estate
Wellingborough
Northants NN8 2QL
Tel: (0933) 225080
Telex: 31428

LAW EXPORT LTD
Quarry Road
Chipping Sodbury
Bristol BS17 6AX
Tel: (0454) 322445
Telex: 44396G

LEE HOWL & CO. LTD
Alexandra Road
Tipton
Midlands DY4 8TA
Tel: 021-557 6161

LISTER, R.A., FARM EQUIPMENT LTD
Long Street
Dursley
Gloucestershire GL11 4HF
Tel: (0453) 4141
Telex: 437152 LISTERG

MAWROB CO. (ENGINEERS) LTD
121a/125a Sefton Street
Southport

Merseyside PR8 5DR
Tel: (0704) 37408

MECHANISED HANDLING
Great Gransden
Sandy
Bedfordshire SG19 3AY
Tel: (076 77) 255

MULTIHOE GARDEN TOOLS
Hayne Barton
Stowford
Lewdown
Devon EX20 4BZ
Tel: (056 683) 311

PROJECT EQUIPMENT LTD
Industrial Estate
Rednal Airfield
West Felton
Oswestry
Salop SY11 4HS
Tel: (069 188) 263

RUSSELLS (KIRBYMOORSIDE) LTD
Kirbymoorside
Yorkshire YO6 6DJ
Tel: (0751) 31381
Telex: 57516 RUSSEL G

SCOTMEC LTD
1 Whitfield Drive
Heathfield
Ayr KAH 9RX
Tel: (0292) 289999
Telex: 778770
Cable: SCOTMEC. AYR

**SELF SUFFICIENCY AND
SMALLHOLDING SUPPLIES**
Little Burcott
Wells
Somerset BA5 1NQ
Tel: (0749) 72127

SOLARPAK LTD
Factory 3
Lock Lane
High Wycombe
Telex: 837383

NEILL TOOLS DIVISION LTD
St. Paul's Road
Wednesbury
W. Midlands WS10 9RA
Tel: 021-556 1414
Telex: 336549
Cable: SPEARTOOLS WEDNESBURY

TINSLEY, E., & CO. LTD
P.O. Box 35
Reddal Hill Road
Cradley Heath
Warley
W. Midlands B64 5JF
Tel: (0384) 66066
Telex: 335249

TUDOR, M.E
Frogmore Cottage
Sawyers Hill
Minety
Nr. Malmesbury
Wilts SN16 9QL
Tel: (0666) 860437

VETERINARY DRUG CO
129-135 Lawrence Street
York YO1 3EG
Tel: (0904) 412314
Telex: 57588 VETORV G

WOLF TOOLS LTD
Ross-on-Wye
Herefordshire HR9 5NE
Tel: (0989) 767600
Telex: 35205

WOLSELEY ENGINEERING PRODUCTS
H. Cameron Gardner Ltd
Bath Road
Woodchester
Stroud
Glos GL5 5EX
Tel: (045 383) 2526
Telex: 437197

WYATT BRO. (WHITCHURCH) LTD
Wayland Works
Whitchurch
Shropshire SY13 1RS
Tel: (0948) 2526

USA

AMERICAN LAWN MOWER CO
705 T.E. 18th Street
P.O. Box 2505
Muncie
IN 47302
Tel: 317 288 6624

HELLER ALLER CO. INC
P.O. Box 29
Corner Perry 7 Oakwood Streets
Napoleon
OH 43545

BELL, C.S., CO
170 W Davis Street
Box 291
Tiffin
OH 44883
Tel: (419) 448 0791

BELLOW'S VALVAIR INTERNATIONAL
200 W Exchange Street
Akron
OH 44309
Tel: (216) 762 0471

DAVIS, H.C., SONS, MFG. CO. INC
P.O. Box 395
Bonner Springs
KS 66012
Tel: (913) 422 3000

DEMPSTER INDUSTRIES INC
P.O. Box 848
Beatrice
NE 68310
Tel: (402) 223 4026
Telex: 724353

EARTHWAY PRODUCTS INC
P.O. Box 547

Maple Street
Bristol
IN 46507
Tel: (219) 848 7491

LAMBERT CORP
P.O. Box 278
Ansonia
OH 45303
Tel: 513 337 3641

SEYMOUR MAN. CO. INC
P.O. Box 248
500 North Broadway
Seymour
IN 47274
Tel: (812) 522 2900
Telex: 276253-C of C SEYM

SWANSON MACHINE CO
20-26 E. Columbia Avenue
Champaign
IL 61820
Tel: (217) 352 2963

W. Germany

AEG TELEFUNKEN
Industriestraße 29
2000 Wedel
Tel: (04103) 7021

AGRIA-WERKE GmbH
Postfach 1147
7108 Möckmühl
Tel: (06298) 5061
Telex: 04 66791
Cable: AGRIA-WERKE

GUTBROD-WERKE GmbH
Postfach 60
6601 Saarbrücken-Bübingen
Tel: (06805) 791
Telex: 4429 119 GUTB D

HAUPTNER, H
Postfach 2201-34
5650 Solingen 1
Tel: (021 22) 5.0075.0
Telex: 8514-409 NAHA D
Cable: VETERINARA

HEGER, MASCHINENFABRIK, GmbH
Zaberstraße 26
7033 Herrenberg 1
Tel: (07032) 31437
Telex: 72 65 467

HINGHAUS MASCHINENFABRIK GmbH
Kampenstraße 9
4804 Versmold/Westf.
Tel: (05423) 7644
Telex: 941724

POLAR WERKE GmbH
Postfach 140460
5639 Remscheid 1
Tel: (02191) 8547
Telex: 08513 687
Cable: POLAR REMSCHEID

PUMPENFABRIK BEYER
Dorfstraße 25
Ot Wulfsfelde
2361 Pronstorf
Tel: (04506) 282
Telex: 261487 BEYER D

RAU, MASCHINENFABRIK, GmbH
Johannes-Rau-Straße
7315 Weilheim an der Teck
Tel: (07023) 121
Telex: 7267717
Cable: MAFARAU

RAUCH LANDMASCHINENFABRIK GmbH
Postfach 1107
Sinzheim 7573
Tel: (07221) 8048
Telex: 0781242 RAUCH D.

**RHEINTECHNIK, WEILAND & KASPAR
KG MASCHINENFABRIK**
Postfach 1170
Hellenpfad
5413 Bendorf/Rhein 1
Tel: (02622) 3061
Telex: 0869 733 REIT D

STANDARD LANDMASCHINEN GmbH
Postfach 1160
Kreis Uelzen
3118 Bad Bevensen
Tel: (05821) 1034
Telex: 09 1236

TIGGES, GEBR., GmbH & CO KG
4740 Oelde 2 Sünninghausen
Tel: (02 520) 501
Telex: 89418

**TRÖSTER, A.J., MASCHINENFABRIK
GmbH & CO. KG**
Postfach 240
6308 Butzbach
Tel: (06033) 4171
Telex: 4184680

Zimbabwe

BULAWAYO STEEL PRODUCTS
8 Ironbridge Road
P.O. Box 1603
Donnington
Bulawayo
Tel: 62671
Telex: 3257 ZW
Cable: BYOSTEEL BULAWAYO